A heavy fog set... McCleary and his friends clung desperately to their rubber raft. The mist seemed filled with the odor of dead fish. Then, about forty feet away, they heard a tremendous splash.

The boys knew that no boat had made the sound. They heard another splash. A sickening odor filled the air.

From out of the fog came a strange, high-pitched squeal. The five young men slipped on their fins and decided to swim for safety. In back of them they could hear splashing and a strange hissing sound.

Suddenly there was a terrible scream that lasted nearly half a minute. "Help me! It's got Brad! I've got to get outta here —" Then the voice was cut off abruptly.

**Other Scholastic paperbacks
you might enjoy:**

BEYOND BELIEF

STRANGE, TRUE MYSTERIES OF THE UNKNOWN

Brad Steiger

SCHOLASTIC INC.
New York Toronto London Auckland Sydney

ISBN 0-590-44252-X

20 19 18 17 16 15 14 13   11 12 13 14 15/0

Printed in the U.S.A.   23

First Scholastic printing, October 1991

Contents

1
The Eerie Enigma
of Ghost Ships

"SOS . . . SOS. . . . " came the frenzied radio call from the Dutch vessel S.S. *Ourang Medan* in February, 1948. "All officers including captain dead . . . probably whole crew. . . . " There followed a series of jumbled dots and dashes and then: "I die."

Rescue ships rushed to the location of the vessel in distress. They found her only a few miles from the position given, in the waters off what are now Malaysia and Sumatra. Boats were launched to investigate.

The rescue parties were greeted by a grotesque sight when they boarded the *Ourang Medan*. The lifeless crew lay everywhere — on the decks, on their bunks, in the passageways. The officers were sprawled in the wheelhouse, the chartroom, and the wardroom. The wireless operator was at his post in the radio shack, his hand still on the sending key. On all of the dead men's faces was a look of convulsive horror, their frozen features upturned, with gaping mouths and staring eyes.

After the stunned rescue parties had recovered from their shock, they examined the corpses more closely, trying to determine the cause of the crew's sudden and bizarre demise. There were no signs of injuries or symptoms of disease on any of the bodies. Yet even the ship's dog was lifeless, its teeth bared in a rage of pain.

As a rescue ship prepared to tow the ill-fated vessel into port, flames suddenly and inexplicably belched forth from the hold. The fire was immediately so widespread that the boarding party quickly abandoned the jinxed ship.

Moments later, the *Ourang Medan* seemed to leap into the air as a terrific explosion racked her metal frame. Then she settled back and slowly slid beneath the water, submerging forever in the depths of the sea any clue as to what had happened to her.

No explanation has ever been given for the crew's death or the *Ourang Medan*'s sudden bursting into flames. But even though the ship sank beneath the waves forty-three years ago, she is still being sighted by seamen in the waters off Malaysia and Sumatra. The *Ourang Medan* has achieved bizarre immortality as a ghost ship.

Ghostly phenomena are not confined to creaking mansions and haunted houses on land, but can be seafaring as well. For four hundred years, ships' logs have recorded the sudden appearances and disappearances of "ships that were not there."

One of the more persistent folk myths of a ghost ship is the ancient tale of Captain Van Dieman and his ship, *The Flying Dutchman*. According to the legend, as punishment for blasphemy, Van Dieman is forever doomed to try in vain to round the Cape of Good Hope, at the tip of Africa. The appearance of *The Flying Dutchman* is considered by seamen to be an omen of disaster. If a lookout man sights her in the morning fog, he is almost certain to suffer an accident by nightfall.

Another phantom ship that acts as a bad omen is the specter of a medieval Chinese pirate vessel that haunts the Yangtze River. It has been reported that she has passed through river craft with her sails billowing when there was not a breath of air and without leaving a ripple to trace her passage. The ghostly pirate ship is said to have heralded wars, famines, and the deaths of thousands.

A similar phantom vessel visits the fishermen of Chileo Island, South America. It is called the *Caleuche*, and the fishermen claim that it leaves floundered craft and drowned men in its wake.

The Curse of Hitler's Yacht

A more direct curse seems to have followed the subsequent owners of Adolf Hitler's yacht, the *Ostwind*. Constructed on the Führer's orders and designed to conquer all comers in international yacht races, the sleek, eighty-five-foot craft was launched just three days after the German Army invaded Poland. Opportunities for yacht racing stopped with the onset of World War II, so rather than let the vessel sit idle, Hitler appropriated the *Ostwind* as his private pleasure boat.

In 1950, several years after the war's end, the U.S. Navy sold the captured vessel to Commander John Lyman, a Navy officer and an avid yachtsman. He entered the *Ostwind* in races up and down the East Coast. But in Miami, a heavy piece of sailing gear mysteriously fell from the rigging and smashed his face. Seriously injured, Lyman sold the *Ostwind* to entrepreneurs who converted the craft into a sleazy imitation of its former majestic appearance.

A Daytona Beach attorney, horrified at the *Ostwind*'s fate, bought the yacht with the intention of restoring its fading glory. The vessel suddenly sank, and the attorney died less than a year later.

In 1971, Horace Glass, a Jacksonville advertising executive, raised the yacht and spent ten years and over $110,000 in an effort to convert the *Ostwind* into a floating museum. But the curse caught up with him in 1982, when a storm undid all of Glass's costly restoration work and left him financially drained.

In 1990, a Miami Beach politician took the rotting hulk out to sea and sank it, sending the curse to the bottom of the ocean along with the *Ostwind*.

A Ghost Ship with Its
Warning Sirens Blasting

In April, 1936, the S.S. *Khosrou*, left Calcutta on her way to Bombay. The weather was rough, and frequently rain poured down. On the return voyage the skies were still heavy, and after several days out on the high seas the *Khosrou* was barely making five knots as it pushed through a torrential downpour.

Under such conditions, the ship's captain was taking no chances. At his command, the sirens were sounded every two minutes.

All at once the sound of another siren echoed that of the *Khosrou*. Immediately all engines were cut, and the ship drifted through the nearly blinding rain. Blast for blast, the two sirens reverberated across the water, but the crewmen of the *Khosrou* searched in vain for the other ship.

Then suddenly the other vessel was sighted off the port bow, looming up out of the mist. She was a motor ship, about 6,000 tons. As the *Khosrou* came within a cable's length of her, the crew was able to read her name clearly: *Tricouleur*.

Strangely enough, to the anxiously scanning eyes of the seamen of the *Khosrou*, the *Tricouleur* appeared to be deserted. No helmsman could be spotted at the wheel. The deck was completely empty.

The *Tricouleur* was in full view of the crew and officers of the *Khosrou* as they glided past her, then she was once again lost in the rainy gloom.

Within minutes of the two ships passing one another, the downpour let up and visibility was restored. The coast of Ceylon could be seen up ahead. In back of them, the men of the *Khosrou* could see for miles.

"Hey!" shouted the first mate in alarm. "Where did the *Tricouleur* go?"

The skipper heard him and wheeled around. There was no trace of the other vessel. Visibility by this time was seven miles. Considering the speed of the two ships and the fact that they had passed only ten minutes before, the *Tricouleur* should have been three miles behind them. The skipper and the mate looked around. Their ship was alone on the sea.

The ship's navigator motioned the officers into the chartroom. "Just behind our position," he said slowly, "about two miles back, there is a symbol labeling the spot of a wreck. Alongside the symbol you can see the notation: 'M.S. *Tricouleur*, with a cargo of chemicals, exploded and sank at this point at 5 P.M., on January 5, 1931.' "

The skipper looked at the chart, then glanced involuntarily at the clock on the wall. It was January 5, 1937, and the time was 5:15 P.M. It was six years to the hour since the wreck of the *Tricouleur* had occurred.

Why do seamen sight ghost ships? Do lookouts spot mysteriously glowing brigs on dark, stormy nights only because tradition says they are *supposed* to see them? Are such phantoms merely hallucinations brought on by lonely days and nights and a craving for a super-event to break the monotony? Or do such eerie appearances point to an even greater mystery, a mystery that stretches far beyond the shores of the deepest and the broadest ocean?

Invaded by a Skeleton
with Long Blonde Hair

In August, 1989, the terrified crew of an Italian fishing boat abandoned ship and refused to set foot on its deck again. Italian Navy Lieutenant Giosue Jacolino, the officer in charge of investigating the incredible incident, said that the ship's captain, Salvatore Giamaglia, confirmed his crew's story that ghosts had invaded their vessel.

Filippo Musumeci, the maintenance engineer for the seventy-five-foot *Francesco*, said that although he had never before believed in ghosts, his recent experiences had forced him to change his mind.

The ghostly invasion had begun with books, bottles, and shoes flying through the air and striking the seamen. Their tools and appliances were tossed about by invisible hands. Although the *Francesco* had a sophisticated automatic pilot, the boat careened through the seas as if piloted by a drunken navigator. The radar showed objects that didn't exist. The crew's watches went berserk, moving the time hours ahead or hours behind.

Then, on the sixth day, a woman's skeleton with long blonde hair materialized and commanded them to leave the boat at once. "Get off this boat!" she shouted at them, "or I'll kill you!"

The crew had had enough. They demanded that Captain Giamaglia take them at once to the nearest port. In a few hours, they had docked at the Greek town of Kastelli.

Unable to shake the seamen's fantastic account of having been terrorized for six days by ghosts, Lieutenant Jacolino vowed to conduct a serious investigation to solve the mystery of this modern ghost ship. But to this day it remains unsolved.

The Flaming Ghost Ship of Bay Chaleur

Inhabitants along Bay Chaleur on the northern shores of New Brunswick continue to sight the mysterious "fire ship" that puzzled their parents and grandparents for nearly a century. In a spring, 1968, article on this floating phantom, the *Hamilton Spectator* in Hamilton, Ontario, reported that although some of the accounts were difficult to credit, it could not deny that many responsible, reliable people have witnessed the phenomenon.

According to most of the reports, a ship swathed in flames appears in Bay Chaleur. Huge tongues of fire shoot up its masts. Against this blazing inferno, which lights up the night sky, burning figures can be seen scrambling in the ship's rigging. The initial reaction of first-time sighters is to put to sea to look for survivors. But those rescuers coming to help the seamen who survived the fiery disaster are rewarded with nothing but empty sea.

These are some of the more popular explanations for the fire ship:

• It is the ghost of a ship whose charred remains are buried under the sand at Green Point. Although this vessel's history is unknown, according to legend it ran aground some three hundred years ago after being burned to the waterline.

• It is the specter of the *John Craig*, a ship whose career ended in tragedy at Shippegan Island.

• The fiery phantom is that of a warship destroyed in the bay during the War of 1812.

• It is the ghost of a ship that put out from a U.S. port, manned by a drunken crew and captained by a partying skipper. The seamen got lost at sea and drifted into Bay Chaleur where a fight broke out in the captain's quarters, causing a lamp to explode. The crew was unable to put out the flames, and everyone on board was killed. Because their drunken negligence caused the loss of their ship, the rowdy skipper and his hard-drinking crew are condemned to wander forever on the waves and to burst into flames in Bay Chaleur again and again throughout eternity.

• It is the phantom of an immigrant ship whose captain sailed into the bay thinking that it was the Gulf of St. Lawrence. While in the bay's waters, the ship was struck by lightning when a storm suddenly arose off the Gaspé coast. In this account, two small boys survived when the ship ran aground at the mouth of the Restigouche River, but all others perished.

According to the *Hamilton Spectator*, Mrs. John Nicol and her next-door neighbors, Mr. and Mrs. Freeman Rogers, have all observed the ghostly "fire ship" of Bay Chaleur. Mrs. Nicol described the phenomenon as "riding the water, but not going anywhere. I don't believe in ghost ships," she added, "but that's what it looked like."

The Rogers family, together with six visitors in their home, watched "flames coming from the outline of a ship" for nearly an hour. Their daughter, Edith, said that she has seen a three-masted vessel "with her sails brilliantly ablaze."

Tales of Vanishing Seamen

Another type of sea specter is that of the perfectly seaworthy vessel drifting with no sign of a crew. Frequently these ships are discovered with everything in order, no evidence of any sort of violence, with the lifeboats still in place and well secured. The question that demands an answer — yet remains forever unanswered — is, *What happened to the crew?* And lurking in the minds of those who discover such abandoned vessels is the fear that whatever did happen to the vanished seamen, it could also happen to them.

In 1850 at Easton's Island, not far from Newport, Rhode Island, local farmers and fishermen looked up from their work one day to see an unusual vessel making for the shore, under full sail, in a stiff breeze. As the ship drew nearer, they saw that there were no seamen on board. Crowds began to gather on the beach, for it was clear that the ship was going to run aground.

Rather than crashing into the shore, however, the ship gently glided up to the beach and came to a clean halt as the astonished witnesses watched in amazement. The crowd immediately clambered on deck and discovered that she was *The Seabird*, under the command of Captain John Huxham. Further searching revealed that she was due in Newport that very day on a return voyage from Honduras.

The Seabird was found to be in perfectly navigable order. Charts and instruments were undisturbed and in excellent condition. Mess had been set out for the crew, and coffee was perking on the galley stove. Yet, with the exception of one mongrel dog, there was no living thing on board the ship.

After extensive investigations, it could only be concluded that *somehow* the captain and his crew had vanished completely from a perfectly sound ship during calm weather.

Mummies Piloted the Ship for Twenty Years

When the mate and several of the crew of a sailing vessel boarded the *Marlborough* in a cove of Tierra del Fuego, off the southern coast of Argentina, in October, 1913, they were completely stunned by the ghastly sight that awaited them. Scattered about the decks were the shrunken and mummified bodies of the ship's passengers and crew.

"It's like a floating tomb," gasped one of the boarding party that was investigating the lifeless ship floating in the cove.

The masts of the *Marlborough* were still intact, but the sails hung in shreds, long since tattered by the merciless forces of wind and water. A green mold covered everything.

"It's the same down below," reported a sailor, who desperately sought to control his nausea. "There's nothing down here but a bunch of mummies."

The mate had gone directly to the master's cabin, seeking a clue to the sea mystery in the ship's log. He found a skeletal captain hunched over the leather binding of a logbook, but its pages had rotted away.

Subsequent investigation uncovered a startling fact: The *Marlborough* had left Lyttelton, New Zealand, in early January, 1890 — nearly *twenty-four years* before her discovery off Tierra del Fuego. The three-masted sailing vessel had been bound for her home port of Glasgow, Scotland. She had carried a mixed cargo, a number of passengers, and a full crew of veteran sailors under the command of Captain Hird, an experienced sea captain. So why had he chosen to sail around South America rather than Africa?

On that day in October, 1913, when the *Marlborough* was discovered, she was soft with rot and spongy with mold. It was clear to the investigators that the *Marlborough* could not have been drifting in that cove for two decades. The furious storms for which Tierra del Fuego is noted would long since have pounded her into splinters.

From all indications, the *Marlborough* had drifted into the cove only a short time before she **was** discovered by the crew of the sailing vessel.

What had happened to the *Marlborough* crew? And how had she managed to keep from crashing into the reefs when every member of her passenger list and crew had apparently been dead for over twenty years?

Vanished Without a Trace
Aboard the *J.C. Cousins*

In 1894, the yacht *J.C. Cousins*, one of the fastest ships in the waters of the Pacific Northwest, made her way through the treacherous shoals and sandbars off the coast of Astoria, Oregon, then anchored off Fort Stevens to await the turning of the tide. The lookout at Cape Disappointment recorded that the *J.C. Cousins* upped anchor at five o'clock and began to make her way gracefully to the open sea.

Suddenly, under the watchful eyes of the coastguardsmen's telescopes, the sleek vessel abruptly came about and cut through the water for shore. To their astonishment, the *J.C. Cousins* continued at full sail until it grounded itself on a sandbar.

Later, on board the craft, coastguardsmen found no signs of struggle or panic. Going below, they found a warm meal prepared for the crew. In an ashtray, a lighted cigar was burning slowly — but there was no sign of its smoker or anyone else.

An inspection of the cabins revealed that all were in order, with no indications of distress. And all were, without exception, devoid of human life.

It was well known that Captain Hans Zeiber was inordinately proud of his eighty-seven-foot twinmasted vessel and would not desert it under *any* circumstances. The ship's log was carefully — but fruitlessly — searched for some clue to the mysterious disappearance of Zeiber and his crew. The sea was scanned. The beaches were checked for weeks for bodies washed ashore. But no one has ever solved the puzzle of the *J.C. Cousins*.

Unknown Forces
That Snatch Entire Ships

Such strange disappearances — and there are dozens like them — have sent generations of investigators to explore macabre mysteries of the sea. While natural explanations have solved some of the cases, a disturbing number remain, refusing to be explained away. Because of all the unsolvable cases of disappearing or abandoned ships, some seamen and researchers argue that there may be certain areas of the oceans that are haunted by unknown and hostile forces.

In February, 1963, the *Marine Sulphur Queen* made a voyage into oblivion. Leaving the port of Beaumont, Texas, on the way to Norfolk, Virginia, she was last heard from on a routine call from the Dry Tortugas in the Gulf of Mexico. When she became overdue in Norfolk, a search party was organized that was later abandoned when no clues were discovered.

Five days after the search had been terminated, a navy torpedo retriever found a lifejacket and some debris believed to be from the ill-fated tanker.

These items were discovered in the Florida straits, fourteen miles southeast of Key West. Nothing else has ever been found.

At 9:00 P.M. on December 24, 1967, the twenty-three-foot inboard-outboard *Witchcraft* radioed a distress signal from a position about one mile east of Miami. The Coast Guard said later that they had been on the scene within twenty minutes, but had been unable to find any trace of the luxury boat. Both the Coast Guard and the Civil Air Patrol spent a full day searching for the craft without success.

The notion that a twenty-three-foot craft could disappear completely — within sight of a major city and within twenty minutes of the Coast Guard's arrival — penetrates the brain with an icy chill.

Men have been disappearing along with their ships since the first primitive seafarers set out from shore astride a log. The fact that such things have been occurring since the dawn of civilization, however, offers little consolation. And it becomes increasingly difficult to accept such mysteries in these days of radio, radar, sonar, and instant aerial search parties.

Are Underwater UFOs Kidnapping Our Planet's Seamen?

A few researchers of these sea mysteries have suggested that UFOs might somehow be responsible. Are there unidentified strangers in our oceans who are kidnapping whole ships and hundreds of seamen?

In the summer of 1969, Englishman John Fairfax rowed his way across the Atlantic, docking in Fort Lauderdale after six harrowing months alone on the sea. Reluctantly, Fairfax told the Fort Lauderdale *News and Sun Sentinel* (July 20, 1969) the most impressive thing that had happened to him during the voyage was a visitation from "flying saucers."

Protesting that he had never believed in such things, Fairfax stated that what he saw could not have been anything else. And his experience consisted of more than simply *observing* UFOs. He felt a force, he told the journalists, as though the flying saucers kept asking him to come with them.

"And I was fighting it and saying back, 'No, no, no,' " Fairfax went on. "It was like telepathy, like being hypnotized."

Could it be that sailors from other vessels, lacking John Fairfax's willpower — or feeling safety in numbers — accepted the aliens' invitation to come with them?

Mark Your Calendars
to Watch a Ghost Ship Appear

As any investigator soon discovers, ghost ships offer far more questions than solutions. But the tragic phantom vessel *Lady Luvibund* also offers a photo opportunity you can mark on your calendars — for it won't be long before it's time for her to appear once again.

According to the legend, on February 13, 1748, a joyous Captain Simon Reed sailed from England bound for Oporto, Portugal, with his bride. The clever seaman had managed to combine business with his honeymoon, and a group of his friends were with him in his cabin celebrating the festive event.

On deck, though, First Mate John Rivers did not share his captain's happiness. In fact, he cursed Simon Reed for marrying the only girl he himself had ever loved. Reed, completely unaware of Rivers's affection for the girl, had even had his first mate stand beside him as best man.

Smoldering in pain and humiliation, Rivers saw his opportunity for revenge as the *Lady Luvibund* approached the Goodwin Sands, a notorious ship's graveyard off the coast of Kent, England. Approaching the helmsman, Rivers told him that he would take over the wheel.

As soon as the deck was clear, Rivers turned the vessel around and headed for shore. While the merry wedding party celebrated below, unaware, the first mate drove the *Lady Luvibund* full speed into the bars and shoals. Trapped below decks, the captain, his bride, and all of their friends perished. In fact, every hand on board died as the ship broke apart on the shoals.

At the inquiry, Rivers's mother revealed her son's love for the captain's wife and his vow for vengeance — even if he should lose his own life in its pursuit. Witnesses on the shore testified that the ship deliberately ran aground.

The tale might have ended then if it had not been

for an angry sea captain's report exactly fifty years later to the day. On February 13, 1798, Captain James Westlake of the coasting vessel *Edenbridge* complained that he had nearly collided with another ship off the Goodwin Sands. He was furious and demanded that the officers of the other ship be arrested. It was obvious, Westlake charged, that there was a party going on that was so boisterous, his crew's warning shouts could not be heard.

When the authorities questioned the neighboring fishermen, they testified that the offending ship had broken up on the shoals as they watched. When they had hurried to the scene, however, they could find no sign of wreckage. The vessel was, the fishermen concluded, a ghost ship.

A half century later, on the same date, the officers and crew of an American schooner watched in horror as the *Lady Luvibund* repeated her desperate plunge to death against the shoals. Once again, when rescue boats were launched, no physical evidence of a wreck could be found.

Fifty years later, in 1898, then again in 1948, local people on shore watched the *Lady Luvibund* repeat her dash to destruction. If all goes according to schedule, spectators who gather on shore on February 13, 1998, will also be able to observe the sorrowful *Lady Luvibund*.

2
Here There Be Sea and Lake Monsters!

". . . My attention was drawn to a large brown fin or frill sticking out of the water, dark seaweed-brown in color, somewhat crinkled at the edge. It was about six feet in length and projected from eighteen inches to two feet from the water. I could see, under the water . . . the shape of a considerable body — a great head and neck . . . came out of the water in front of it . . . The neck appeared to be the thickness of a slight man's body, and from seven to eight feet was out of the water. . . . The head [and eyes] had a very turtle-like appearance. . . . It moved its neck from side to side in a peculiar manner. . . ." (From a paper presented to the Zoological Society of Britain by E.G.B. Meade-Waldo on June 19, 1906.)

On January 13, 1852, Captain Seabury, master of the whaler *Monongahela*, spotted, through his telescope, a monstrous creature thrashing about in agony. Three longboats were sent over the side to end the beast's misery. As a harpoon struck home, a nightmarish head almost ten feet long rose out of the water and lunged at the boats. Two of the longboats were capsized in seconds.

A heavy line snaked over the bow of the ship as the creature sounded and dove for the bottom. More than a thousand feet of line went out before the monster ceased its descent. The *Rebecca Sims*, under the command of Captain Samuel Gavitt, pulled alongside her sister ship to discuss the strange and frightening beast.

By the next morning, the massive carcass had popped to the surface. It was much longer than the *Monongahela*, which measured over one hundred feet from bow to stern. The great sea beast had a body about fifty feet in diameter. Its neck was ten feet wide and supported a huge alligatorlike head ten feet long. The whalers counted ninety-four teeth in its terrible jaws. The saberlike teeth were each about three inches long and hooked backward like those of a snake. The gigantic sea creature was brownish-gray with a light stripe about three feet wide running its full length.

When the practical seamen tried to render the creature as if it were a whale, they were disappointed to find that the behemoth possessed only a tough skin and no blubber.

Captain Seabury ordered the monster's head to be severed and placed in a huge pickling vat. He was well aware of the ridicule heaped upon those seamen who claimed to have seen sea serpents, and he was determined to bring back proof of the creature's existence. In addition to the hideous trophy, Captain Seabury wrote out a complete report of the death of the beast and included a lengthy description of the monster.

Captain Seabury gave his report to the homeward-bound *Rebecca Sims*. Unfortunately for science and for all maligned sighters of sea monsters, he did not deliver the serpent's head into Captain Gavitt's keeping as well. The *Monongahela* never made its way back to New Bedford with its fantastic prize. Many years later her name board was found on the shore of Umnak Island in the Aleutians.

Many skeptics believe that only superstitious seamen of long ago saw sea monsters, and that with sea traffic now so heavy, if sea monsters really existed, one surely would have been caught.

But sea monsters are *not* just things of the past. Large, unidentifiable creatures of serpentine appearance and incredible proportions continue to be spotted. And even with increased sea traffic, improved sailing vessels, and modern technology, these massive monsters still elude capture. There are, however, a number of earnest, scientifically trained, and technologically equipped sea serpent and lake monster hunters who insist that it may not be too far in the future before Sea World will feature real-life sea monsters for a Sunday afternoon's viewing. If such a capture should soon take place, one thing is certain: Sea World will need a tank even larger than Shamu the whale's in which to keep the thing.

Late in March, 1969, two fishermen angling off the City Island Bridge near the Bronx, New York, claimed to have seen a giant sea creature moving in the deep channel used by oil tankers that travel up the Hutchinson River. The fishermen described the monster as black and gray and bigger than any living thing they had ever seen.

Harbor police who investigated found nothing, but they were soon called to Long Island Sound to look into a similar report from Little Neck Bay, Queens. Something larger than a whale, something that could not be identified by longtime fishermen with practiced eyes, was exploring the bays of New York City.

At about the same time, on the other side of the world, North American Newspaper Alliance reporters were writing the story told by fourteen Hong Kong university students who saw a "big, black creature with green eyes" staring at them from only twenty yards offshore.

According to Benjamin Chae, the students had heard a crying noise coming from the sea. When one of the girls screamed, Chae looked out to the ocean and saw "a big, black creature rising from the water." Chae yelled out, *"Kai Kwai"* [sea devil], and all the other students ran up to the shoreline and saw the thing, too.

The Hong Kong university students estimated

that the monster was twenty to thirty feet in length, and they insisted that the creature made a loud, crying noise. In their opinion, it was definitely not a fish.

On March 7, 1969, a massive "something" washed up on a Mexican beach. At first it was declared to be the remains of some prehistoric creature that had been thawed out of a drifting iceberg. Later, two biologists at the Mexican Navy's marine biology station at Tampico announced that the hulk was an oversized sperm whale. Other scientists disagreed, pointing to the thing's horn and shoulder blade as evidence that it could hardly be a whale of any kind.

The behemoth was dragged ashore with the aid of tractors and more than one hundred fishermen and soldiers tugging on cables tied to its carcass. An estimate of its weight was made difficult by the mutilations of sharks and by superstitious fishermen. But tests indicated that the unidentified monster had once weighed somewhere between twelve and thirty-five tons.

All devoted monster hunters can only wish that actor-producer Cornel Wilde's cameramen had had more nimble fingers when they were shooting the war epic *Beach Red* in the Philippines. If they had been quicker, we might be in possession of a strip of film showing a rather vicious sea serpent *in action*.

Harrison Carroll told of the experience in his column in the Los Angeles *Herald-Examiner*, December 27, 1966: "They were shooting off Bauang. . . . After the firing of some underwater charges, some kind of a giant sea monster surfaced beside the boats. They said it had the flat head of [a] snake and a long serpent-like body. While the men were trying to get it aboard a boat, it bit the steel shaft off an underwater spear. That ended that. The monster sank again into the water."

A Fatal Sea Monster Attack
for Four Teenagers

One of the more frightening personal encounters with a sea monster was relayed by teenaged Edward Brian McCleary, who said that his nightmarish story began on the pleasant Saturday morning of March 24, 1962, in Pensacola Bay, Florida. McCleary and four friends — Eric, Warren, Brad, and Larry — had been skin-diving near the sunken *Massachusetts* when a sudden storm sent them into the ocean.

After the squall had let up, a heavy fog settled over the sea, and the five boys clung desperately to their rubber raft. The mist seemed filled with the odor of dead fish. Then, about forty feet away, they heard a tremendous splash. Waves reached the raft and broke over the side.

Whatever it was, the boys knew that no boat had made the sound. They heard another splash, and through the fog they could make out what looked like a ten-foot pole with a bulbous head on top. It remained erect for a moment, then bent in the middle and dove under the surface. A sickening odor filled the air.

From out of the fog came a strange, high-pitched squeal. The five young men panicked, slipped on their fins, and decided to keep together and swim for the portion of the wrecked *Massachusetts* that remained above water. In back of them, as they swam, they could hear splashing and a strange hissing sound.

McCleary remembered hearing a terrible scream that lasted for nearly half a minute. "I heard Warren call, 'Help me! It's got Brad! I've got to get outta here — ' Then Warren's voice was cut off abruptly by a short cry."

The three remaining swimmers clustered together, not knowing how many feet of ocean separated them from whatever monster was down there waiting for them.

Larry was the next to disappear. One minute he was there beside them; the next, he was gone.

The two boys dove for their friend, but found nothing. Eric got a cramp in his leg. McCleary wrapped his arm around Eric's neck, and they continued toward the wreck.

A wave broke, separating them. When McCleary surfaced, he saw Eric swimming ahead of him.

What happened next is the stuff of which lifelong nightmares are made.

"Right next to Eric that telephone-pole-like figure broke water," McCleary stated later to the authorities. "I could see the long neck and two small eyes. The mouth opened, and [the monster] bent over. It dove on top of Eric, dragging him under. I screamed and began to swim past the ship. My insides were shaking uncontrollably."

Somehow the teenage boy managed to swim the remaining two miles to shore. He later recalled fragmentary images of sprawling on the beach, stumbling to a tower of some sort, and falling on his face before a group of boys. When he regained consciousness, he was in the Pensacola Naval Base hospital.

None of the reporters told all the facts of his escape from the hideous sea beast that took the lives of his four friends. Each of the various local newspapers carried the story of the tragedy, but they all attributed the boys' deaths to accidental drownings. McCleary was told that his story about the sea serpent was best left unmentioned.

It remained for Edward Brian McCleary to write his own account for *Fate*, a small circulation magazine that specializes in stories of the strange, the unusual, and the unknown. In his article (May, 1965) he asked E.E. McGovern, the director of the search and rescue units, if he believed that the boys had been attacked by a sea monster. "People don't believe these things because they are afraid to," McGovern admitted. "I believe you, but there's not much else I can do."

The Maine Lobstermen and the Sea Serpent's Skull

On Monday, August 7, 1967, the Gagne brothers — Peter and Richard — of Biddeford, Maine, hauled up a partial skeleton of the oddest-looking thing they'd ever seen.

The Gagne brothers are lobstermen, and Richard pulled up the skeletal remains off the southern coast of Maine. It appeared to be a snakelike head and neck of some undetermined creature over eight feet long.

Peter remarked that the eye sockets on the head were so large that he could put his fist in each one of them. The eyes were on the sides of the head, like a snake's. Bits of flesh still clung to some of the vertebrae.

The story and accompanying pictures of the skeleton were widely circulated by United Press International. Many people who came to view the remains agreed with the Gagnes that the thing looked "just exactly like what a sea monster ought to look like."

The Sea Serpent That Surfaced for a Scientist

The unidentified sea serpent that appeared off the New Jersey coast on August 19, 1963, could not have had a more appreciative or analytical audience. As reported in *The New York Times*, the initial sighting of the creature was made by Dr. Lionel A. Walford, director of the Fish and Wildlife Research Center of the United States Department of the Interior at Sandy Hook, New Jersey.

Dr. Walford cautioned the reporter not to say that he had seen a "sea serpent," but he did provide an excellent description of whatever it was he had seen: "It was at least forty feet in length and about five inches thick and perhaps seven to eight inches deep — looking something like an enormously long, flattened eel."

Dr. Walford finally made a tentative identification of the "serpent" as a Venus Girdle, a jellylike creature. But later, after he had examined his scientific references, he found that the Venus Girdle does not grow longer than a few feet. "No amount of research I could do provided me with a proper identification of this very strange creature," he conceded.

A Sixty-Foot Sea Monster off Nantucket Island

On May 12, 1964, three men aboard the Norwegian fishing boat *Blue Sea* reported that they had seen a sixty-foot sea monster near Nantucket Island. Alf Wilhemsen was the first to sight the creature, and he yelled at his brother Jens and his partner Bjarne Houghan to look at the gigantic serpent swimming a few hundred feet away from their eighty-foot boat.

According to the Norwegians, the monster had a head like an alligator with a lobsterlike tail. Its body was dotted with black and white spots, and it had a series of humps on its otherwise smooth back.

When the fishermen sailed into New Bedford harbor to report their remarkable sighting to the U.S. Bureau of Commercial Fisheries, Coast Guard vessels and fishing boats set out to search for the huge serpent. Three days later, the monster was spotted by the crew of the dragger *Friendship* in an area about ten miles from where the Norwegians had first seen it.

The *Friendship* circled the massive creature twice so that the crew could get a good look at it. Captain Albert Pike gave a description of the alligator-headed serpent that exactly matched the one given by the Norwegians. The monster swam at a speed of five knots and didn't submerge once during the twenty minutes in which it was under observation by the *Friendship*. Unfortunately, the crewmen did not bring the sixty-foot sea beast back to shore, but they did add another well-attested sighting to the annals of sea serpent lore.

Are Sea Serpents Survivors from the Age of Reptiles?

Some scientists who have seriously studied the subject of sea monsters have suggested that the creatures might be surviving members of one of the species of giant sea reptiles of the Mesozoic age, 65 million years ago. No one has yet to offer a completely satisfactory explanation for the rather rapid extinction of the giant reptiles — dinosaurs on the land, pterosaurs in the air, and massive, multi-tonned ichthyosaurs and plesiosaurs in the sea.

The nineteenth-century naturalist Philip Gosse used the plesiosaur theory to explain the sea serpent. Gosse argued that although the Mesozoic age had ended tens of millions of years ago, there was no reason why descendants of the great sea reptiles could not have survived in the oceans.

Our own century has produced evidence that supports Gosse's theory. For example, several crossopterygian fish have been brought up in nets off southeast Africa. These creatures had survived almost unchanged for seventy million years *before* the Age of Reptiles.

Other scientists suggest that "sea serpents" may in fact be giant eels. Dr. Maurice Burton points out in his book *Living Fossils* that in recent years eel larvae three feet long have been discovered. Burton states that if one compares the relative lengths of larvae and full-grown eels that are normal-sized, there is no reason why such giant larvae should not reach lengths of 36 feet when full grown.

At the beginning of the 1960s, Dr. Anton Brun of the University of Copenhagen, Denmark, announced the finding of an eel larvae more than 6 feet long with 450 vertebral plates. The only known eels have but 105 vertebral plates. Dr. Brun, once again working with the comparative sizes of larvae and adults in eels of normal size, reasoned that the larva could easily mature into a monster 90 feet long and weighing several tons.

Other marine zoologists believe that sea monsters are actually some type of undiscovered aquatic mammal related to the whales. They contend that the hairy manes and flippers so often reported on the "serpents" would not appear on reptiles. They also argue that only a warm-blooded mammal would be able to survive in the icy waters of the North Atlantic where so many of the classic sea monster stories have originated.

Still other zoologists suggest that an ancient species of whale, the aeuglodon or basilosaurus, whose fossil remains are well known, would be equipped for the role of sea monster. Basilosaurus is known to have been a huge beast with a slim, elongated body measuring over seventy feet in length. Its skull was long and low, and it propelled itself by means of a single pair of fins located at its forward end.

Basilosaurus is known to have survived into the Miocene epoch, just over thirty million years ago. If crossopterygian fish have survived for more than seventy million years, it seems quite possible a basilosaurus could still be inhabiting our seas.

But what monsters inhabit our lakes?

"Nessie" — Scotland's Favorite Monster

After centuries of keeping an eye out for "Nessie" (Saint Columba made the first recorded sighting in 565 A.D.), solid scientific evidence continues to build proving that the legendary monster of Loch Ness is not just a legend. For years now, volunteer monster-watchers have worked in relays from mid-May to mid-October. Each volunteer is equipped with log pads, field glasses, and video cameras with telephoto lenses. Whenever anyone snaps anything, the film is sent off to the Defense Ministry's Joint Air Reconnaissance Center for careful analysis. This is the same group of experts who in 1943 successfully pinpointed secret Nazi rocket bases from aerial reconnaissance pictures.

Although many interesting photos of "something" in the loch have been taken, among the most convincing remain those taken by the late Tim Dinsdale. On January 24, 1966, the Royal Air Force issued its analysis of the Dinsdale filmstrip. The evaluation focuses on the "hump" of the creature and determines that it is moving at a speed of about ten miles per hour. After much technical discussion about the size and perspective of the "solid, black approximately triangular shape" (the hump) and a comparison of the unidentified creature with a motorboat moving in the same area (filmed immediately after the supposed Nessie had swum past), the RAF states that the object is *not* a surface vessel." And: "One can presumably rule out the idea that it is any sort of submarine vessel for various reasons, which leaves the conclusion that it probably is an animate object."

In 1968, Professor Roy P. Mackal, University of Chicago biologist, became head of the American branch of the Loch Ness Phenomena Investigation Bureau. Professor Mackal has theorized that the type of creature that most fits the evidence and photos of Nessie is some kind of large aquatic mammal capable of thriving above fifty degrees north latitude.

The water in Loch Ness is filled with floating particles of peat and becomes a murky brown just a few feet down. This makes all the standard underwater exploration techniques relatively useless.

In August, 1968, however, a team of sonar experts may have had success in providing evidence that a family of monsters does indeed inhabit the murky waters of the loch. David Tucker, head of the electronic engineering department at Birmingham University, published the results of two weeks of sonar probing in the British journal *New Scientist*. In one thirteen-minute period, Tucker wrote, sonar echoes defined large objects moving underwater. A massive object was recorded swimming at a speed as high as 17 miles per hour, and diving at a rate of 450 feet a minute.

"From the evidence we have," said Tucker, "there is some animal life in the loch whose behavior is difficult to reconcile with that of fish. . . . It is a temptation to suppose the echoes must be the fabulous Loch Ness Monsters."

Dr. Roy Mackal, after years of researching the Loch Ness creature and similar reports of long-necked lake monsters all around the Northern Hemisphere, ventures his opinion that the primitive creatures belong to small, remnant bands of zeuglodons, a primitive ancestor of the whale, long thought to be extinct. The zeuglodons, Dr. Mackal believes, migrate from oceans to lakes, following such prey as spawning salmon. Lake Champlain, with its famous sea monster, "Champ," is linked to the Atlantic Ocean by the Richelieu and St. Lawrence rivers of Quebec. Loch Ness is connected to the sea, and so is Lake Okanagan in British Columbia, where "Ogo Pogo" has frequently been sighted.

"The zeuglodon bear little resemblance to modern whales," Dr. Mackal told the *Boston Globe* on June 28, 1981, pointing out that remains of the alledgedly prehistoric creatures are preserved at the Smithsonian Institute. "It looks like a big anaconda [a semiaquatic boa constrictor] with a ridge down its back."

"Champ," the Monster of Lake Champlain

It has always seemed quite fitting that the first white man to see Champ, the Lake Champlain monster, was the explorer Samuel de Champlain, for whom the lake, which separates Vermont and New York, is named. In his journal entry for July 1609, he describes his observation of a serpentine creature about twenty feet long, as thick as a barrel, with a horselike head. The Indians, he stated, referred to the monster as *Chousaurou*. In the 382 years since the French explorer had his encounter with the strange, unknown beast, there have been hundreds of sightings of Champ.

Beginning in 1974, junior high school teacher Joseph W. Zarzynski has spent a great deal of time and his personal income seeking the creature. In his book *Champ — Beyond the Legend* (1984), Zarzynski makes a strong plea to safeguard the unknown serpentlike creature that he believes lives in the 109-mile lake. Zarzynski admits that most reported sightings of Champ are simply honest misinterpretations of natural lake creatures. However, he argues that the number of *authentic* sightings suggest that Champ is "either a reptile or a mammal, possibly with prehistoric heritage."

In February, 1982, cryptozoologist Loren Coleman revealed in *Boston* magazine that a photograph of Champ taken by a woman with a Kodak Insta-matic camera appeared to have captured the gen-uine image of the lake monster. In the analysis conducted by scientists at the University of Arizona Optical Sciences Center, Dr. B. Roy Frieden, pro-fessor of optical sciences, stated: "The object ap-pears to belong to the photo. We don't see any evidence of tampering with the photo."

J. Richard Greenwell, a researcher at the Uni-versity of Arizona, expressed his opinion that the creature in the photograph appeared to be a "classic *plesiosaur*," an order of seagoing reptiles thought to have become extinct millions of years ago.

"Ogo Pogo" and Other Lake Longnecks

The lakes in the great group including Lakes Manitoba and Winnipegosis have had a long, con-tinuing history of something big and strange fright-ening local fishermen. In the Canadian Rockies, extending into Montana and Idaho, there are lit-erally dozens of lakes associated with monstrous water animals, in the myths, legends, and folklore of Native Americans.

The late Ivan T. Sanderson, a longtime monster hunter, listed Ogo Pogo, the mysterious resident of Lake Okanagan in British Columbia; the *Ta-Zam-a* and the *Tsinquaw* of Lakes Sushwap and Cowichan in the same area; and the "Oogle-Boogles" of Lakes Waterton and Flathead in Montana among the more famous North American water monsters. According to the zoologist-writer, accounts of the Oogle-Boogles have been recorded for decades. Some witnesses have reported creatures with lengths of up to sixty feet.

Most of these unidentified swimming things are described as having "cowlike" heads that sit at the end of long, slender necks with humps behind — hence the nickname, "Longnecks." And there is growing evidence that these creatures exist in nearly every country in the world.

A Man-eating Monster in Siberia's Lake Vororta

There also seem to be *Russian* Longnecks, such as the one that was said to have terrorized Siberia's Lake Vororta some years back. According to reports, the monster ate a swimming dog, a reindeer, and an undetermined number of human beings.

Geologist Viktor Tverdokhlebov recalled for United Press International a lake monster that he had seen in Siberia's Lake Labynikir in 1953:

"It was an ominous-looking dark gray sphere that showed slightly above the water. It inspired nearly uncontrollable fear as it approached. There were two bulging protrusions that must have been eyes approximately seven feet apart on the head.

"The creature reached the bank, stopped, then went into a series of convulsions that raised waves as it disappeared below. There was no question about the monster's intentions. It was heading straight for us, and only when the ripple of water it had stirred reached our feet was its terrible hypnotic spell broken. We were able to flee the water and escape not a moment too soon!"

No such things as sea serpents and lake monsters? They may not really be "serpents," and their size may from time to time become rather exaggerated. But how many of us would have stayed in the water to face down the creature from which Viktor Tverdokhlebov and his friends so wisely fled?

3
Giant Birds, Beasts, and Human Skeletons of Great Size

Sometime in the 1840s, Professor John Russell of Jersey County, Illinois, set out with a guide to explore the cave on the north bank of the Mississippi River that various Indian tribes regarded as the lair of the *Piasa*, a gigantic flying monster with an appetite for human flesh. Russell wrote in his report:

> "The roof of the cavern was vaulted. The top was about twenty feet high. The shape of the cave was irregular, but so far as I could judge, the bottom would average 20 to 30 feet. *The floor of the cave throughout its whole extent was one mass of human bones*. Skulls and other bones were mingled together in the utmost confusion. To what depth they extended I am unable to decide, but we dug to the depth of three or four feet in every quarter of the cavern and still found only bones. *The remains*

of thousands of humans must have been deposited there."

Is it possible that the Piasa of Native American legend was actually a surviving pterodactyl from the Age of Reptiles? Or was it, as one missionary suggested, the "twin brother of Satan"?

Father Marquette, a Jesuit priest-explorer, was among the first white men to view the startling murals that some artist from a forgotten tribal culture had painted on a high bluff of the Mississippi. The two murals, each about thirty feet in length and twelve feet in height, depicted two hideous, gigantic, winged monsters. In his journals of discoveries, published in Paris in 1681, the priest wrote: "As we were descending the river we saw high rocks with hideous monsters painted on them and upon which the bravest Indian dare not look. They [have] head and horns like a goat; their eyes are red; [they have a] beard like a tiger's and a face like a man's. Their tails are so long that they pass over their bodies and between their legs under their bodies, ending like a fish's tail. They are painted red, green, and black . . ."

The two enormous murals were clearly visible on the north bank of the Mississippi where the Illinois State Prison was later built at Alton. Traces of their outlines remained until the limestone on which they had been engraved was quarried by the convicts in about 1856.

In his forty-eight-page booklet, *The Piasa or The Devil Among the Indians* (Morris, Illinois, 1887),

P.A. Armstrong described the creatures as having ". . . the wings of a bat, but of the shape of an eagle's. . . . They also had four legs, each supplied with eagle-shaped talons." Armstrong commented that the creatures were a "blending together of the master species of the earth, sea, and air . . . so as to present the leading and most terrific characteristics of the various species." This combination "is an absolute wonder and seems to show a vastly superior knowledge of animal, fowl, reptile, and fish."

Whatever the murals truly represented, all the American Indian nations of what was then the Northwest Territory told of terrible monsters called the *Piasa* or *Piusa*. According to the legends, the frightening creature would snatch tribespeople and make off with them.

Professor John Russell published an account of the Piasa's insatiable hunger for human flesh in the July, 1848, issue of *The Evangelical Magazine and Gospel Advocate:*

"[The Piasa] would dart suddenly and unexpectedly upon an Indian, bear him off into one of the caves on the bluff and devour him. Hundreds of warriors attempted for years to destroy him, but without success. Whole villages were nearly depopulated, and consternation spread through all tribes of the Illini."

At about the same time that the Piasa was preying on the American Indians along the Mississippi, one of its cousins may have been attacking the Mayans in Mexico. The November, 1968, issue of *Sci-*

ence Digest carried a startling report by Mexican archaeologist-journalist José Diaz-Bolio about his discovery of an ancient Mayan relief sculpture of a peculiar serpent-bird. The sculpture was found in the ruins of Tajin, located in the northeastern section of Veracruz, Mexico; and Diaz-Bolio theorized that the flying serpent was not "merely the product of Mayan flights of fancy, but a realistic representation of an animal that lived during the period of the ancient Mayans — 1,000 to 5,000 years ago."

According to the legends of the Indians of the Illini, after a month of fasting and prayer a resourceful chief named Watogo received instructions from the Great Spirit that enabled him to kill the fearful beast. Watogo, willing to die for his tribe, presented himself as a victim so that his best bowmen could shoot poisoned arrows into the flying monster as it swooped toward him. The Master of Life, in recognition of Watogo's generous deed, held an invisible shield over him, and the Piasa uttered a wild, fearful scream and died.

But did the brave Watogo remember to smash all of the Piasa's eggs?

On April 9, 1948, a farm family outside of Caledonia, Illinois, saw a "monster bird . . . bigger than an airplane." A Freeport truck driver said that he, too, had seen the creature on the same day. A former army colonel admitted that he had spotted it while he stood talking with the head of Western Military Academy and a farmer near Alton, Illinois. "It was a bird of tremendous size," the colonel said.

On April 10, several witnesses saw the gigantic

bird. "I thought it was a type of plane I had never seen before," one witness said. "It was circling and banking in a way I had never seen a plane perform. I kept waiting for it to fall."

On April 24, back at Alton, a man reported he had seen an "enormous, incredible thing . . . flying at about 500 feet and casting a shadow the same size as that of a Piper Cub at the same height." Two policemen said that the creature was "as big as a small airplane."

Are there any known winged giants that could account for these sightings? There are two categories of birds to consider: largest by wingspread and largest by weight. The wandering albatross takes top honors in the first category, sporting a wingspread of twelve feet and a weight of fifteen pounds at its largest. Both the South American and Californian condors are easy winners in the weight category, weighing thirty-one pounds, with a wingspread of eleven feet. For flightless birds, the African ostrich pushes aside all competitors at a height of eight feet and a weight of 160 pounds.

The most massive prehistoric bird was the *Diatryma gigantea* from the lower Eocene of Wyoming. This heavyweight ancestor of today's cranes had a skull almost twenty inches long and a fearsome beak equally long. Standing at seven feet, it had a massive bulk of three hundred pounds.

There seems to be almost no existing culture that does not have its own accounts of Piasas: dragonlike flying monsters that swoop down to snatch victims in grasping talons, or to feast on human sacrifices until a tribal hero arrives to slay them. Some researchers theorize that a certain number of giant reptiles may have survived into the modern era. Another explanation is that various areas on the planet somehow serve as "doorways" to other dimensions of time and space. Perhaps there are ruptures between dimensions that permit monsters from prehistory such as pterodactyls and pleiosaurs to enter and leave our present dimension. If there are such "doorways," then it would seem that one exists around Alton, Illinois, where sightings of a flying reptilian monster have been made hundreds of years apart.

Did Brontosaurus-type Great Reptiles Survive in Africa?

Early in January, 1970, the London Express News Service carried an item about a set of cave paintings that were discovered in the Gorozamzi Hills in what was then called Rhodesia (now Zimbabwe). According to the report, the paintings included a very accurate representation of a brontosaurus (now called apatasaurus), a sixty-seven-foot, thirty-ton behemoth that scientists insist became extinct millions of years before the existence of human life.

Experts agreed that the paintings had been made by bushmen who ruled that area from about 1500 B.C. until a few hundred years ago. They also agreed that the bushmen only painted from life, a belief that is borne out by the other Gorozamzi Hills cave paintings of elephants, hippos, deer, and giraffes.

According to the news story: "The brontosaurus, a member of the dinosaur family, can be seen clearly on the rock, its long neck reaching out of a picture of a swamp . . . Rhodesian museum authorities refuse to believe that the brontosaurus lived in Rhodesia in recent times, for all the fossilized remains they have examined have been millions of years old."

But for at least two hundred years stories have emerged from the swampy jungles of the Ubangi-Congo basin of central Africa about a brownish-gray, elephant-sized creature with a reptilian tail and a long, flexible neck. The native residents call it *mokele-mbembe* (the one who stops the flow of rivers) or *emela-ntuka* (the one who eats the tops of palm trees).

On November 28, 1981, Herman Regusters, an aerospace engineer from South Pasadena, and his wife, Kia, photographed a dinosaurlike reptile as being dark red in color with a long, thick neck, and longer in size than two hippopotamuses.

Unfortunately, the photograph of the creature was quite fuzzy, and the Regusters's tape recording of the "huge, roaring, trumpeting noise" heard frequently around Lake Tele was impossible to identify. Regardless of his lack of definitive physical evidence, Regusters stated that he believed the huge animal to resemble a brontosaurus: "It is 30 feet long. The skin appears slick and smooth. It has a long neck and small snakelike head."

Dr. Roy Mackal, a "monster-hunter" with very impressive academic credentials, led an expedition to the African swamps that are *mokele-mbembe*'s home. In December, 1981, he told news reporters that the native people's descriptions of the creature would fit that of the giant plant-eating reptiles that supposedly became extinct about 60 million years ago.

Of the prehistoric reptiles, the diplodocus was probably the longest, due to its excessively long tail, but the apatasaurus was undoubtedly the heavyweight champ at thirty-eight tons.

Of the present known giants of the animal kingdom, the largest is the African bull elephant, which may stand as high as eleven feet and weigh six to eight tons. The nearest runner-up in size is the Indian elephant, which averages half a foot shorter and a ton lighter than its African cousin.

In the past, a particular European variety of mammoth topped the African elephant by thirty inches, and another extinct elephant rose ten inches taller than the mammoth. Far and away the largest land mammal of all time was the hornless rhinoceros, which lived in southern Asia 65 millions years ago. This beast stood eighteen feet high and reached a length of twenty-seven feet.

The marine mammals of our own day hold the record for gigantic size, exceeding in length and weight everything that has ever lived or breathed. The largest of these creatures, the blue whale, has been recorded as having a length of 100 feet and a weight of 150 tons.

Our modern era has no giants in the reptilian category that can equal the great reptiles of the past. But few swimmers would find the Indian crocodile a delight to encounter as an uninvited water companion. One specimen was measured at thirty-three feet in length and nearly fourteen feet in circumference. The great sea turtles can reach an overall length of nine feet by six and one-half feet, and can weigh as much as 1,450 pounds. The South American anaconda, the largest living snake, uncoils to a length of twenty to twenty-five feet.

A startling *local* giant beast was discovered in Fort Lauderdale, Florida, on August 17, 1989. A 20-foot long, 250-pound python was dragged from beneath a beachfront home. Officials said that the creature might have been prowling the neighborhood after dark for as many as fifteen years, subsisting on raccoons and small domestic pets.

Giant Humans from a Forgotten Prehistoric Past

And what of our own species as monsters and giants? We average a height of five and one-half feet and a weight of 130 pounds, with extremes as tall as eight and one-half feet and as heavy as 600 pounds. We boast an average arm spread of five to eight feet. There is an astonishing amount of evidence to demonstrate that giant humans may have existed in some long-ago forgotten time.

In his January 6, 1973, "Tolbert's Texas" column in the *Dallas Morning News*, Frank X. Tolbert told of the footprint of what might have been a "large humanoid" that was discovered in the Paluxy River. The print measured twenty-one and one-half inches in length, eight inches in width across the front of the foot, and five and one-half inches across the instep. Dr. C.N. Dougherty of Glen Rose, Texas, stated that near the footprint are also the deeply impressed prints of three-toed dinosaurs.

"These men-tracks belong to the Mesozoic era because the clearest man-track is exactly eight inches from a trachodon track and on the same layer of rock," said Dr. Dougherty.

Columnist Tolbert comments that the footprints — and others like them discovered in the Paluxy River — "could have been made by very big human beings," who lived at the same time as the giant reptiles that lived millions of years ago. The thing that most intrigued the journalist is that each of the man-tracks uncovered are twenty-one and one-half inches in length and it appears that "these men who were contemporaries of the brontosaurus, if men they were, walked with a stride of seven feet."

American Indian Legends of the "Allegwi"

Were there truly giants striding across the Americas in our prehistoric past?

According to their oral tradition, the Delaware Indians once lived in the western United States. At some point in their history they migrated eastward as far as the Mississippi River, where they were joined by the Iroquois Confederacy. Both groups of people were seeking better land, and they continued together on their eastward trek.

Scouts who had been sent ahead of the tribes learned of a nation that lived east of the Mississippi who had built strong, walled cities. These people were known as the Talligewi and Allegewi, after whom the Allegheny River and Mountains are named. The Allegewi were much taller than either the Iroquois or the Delaware, and the scouts saw many giants walking among them.

When the two migrating tribes requested permission to pass through the land of the Allegewi, it was denied. Bitter fighting broke out, which continued for many years. Eventually, because there were more Iroquois and Delaware Indians, and they had greater determination, they succeeded in forcing the Allegewi to flee west.

The Allegewi next appear in the legends of the Sioux, whose tradition tells of a confrontation with a people who were "great of stature, but very cowardly." The able and resourceful Sioux warriors exterminated the Allegewi when the giants sought to settle in what is now Minnesota.

Excavating Human Skeletons of Enormous Size

Is there any archaeological evidence to support these Indian legends and traditions?

Rising out of the prairies and meadows in Ohio, Minnesota, Iowa, and other states are the huge earthworks of the mysterious "moundbuilders." Scattered throughout the Midwest, the mounds were apparently raised by the same unknown people.

But do giant mounds indicate giant people?

Enormous weapons, including a copper axe weighing thirty-eight pounds, have been found in some of the mounds. However, outsized weapons, implements, and huge monuments are not proof of a giant race. They could be religious objects or works of art. The best proof of a race of giants would be the discovery of their skeletons.

Several years ago, two brothers living in Dresbach, Minnesota, decided to enlarge their brick business. To do so, they were forced to remove a number of large Indian mounds. In one of the huge earthworks they removed the bones of "men over eight feet tall."

In La Crescent, not far from Dresbach, mound excavators reportedly found huge skillets and bones of "men of huge stature." Over in Chatfield, mounds were uncovered that revealed six skeletons of enormous size. Unusually large skeletons of seven people buried head down were discovered in Clearwater. The skulls in the latter excavation were said to have had receding foreheads and double rows of teeth.

Other discoveries in Minnesota included "men of more than ordinary size" in Moose Island Lake; a skeleton of "gigantic size" in Pine City; and ten skeletons "of both sexes and of gigantic size" in Warren.

Could these huge skeletons of gigantic Indians have been those of the last members of a once proud and majestic prehistoric race? Later, with their numbers severely reduced, their great walled cities destroyed, they may have seemed cowardly to more aggressive tribes such as the Sioux.

On December 2, 1930, *The New York Times* carried an item about the discovery of the remains of an apparent race of giants, at Sayopa, a mining town three hundred miles south of the Mexican border. A mining engineer, J.E. Coker, said that laborers clearing ranchland near the Yazui River "dug into an old cemetery where bodies of men, averaging eight feet in height, were found buried tier by tier. . . ."

On February 14, 1936, *The New York Times* ran a piece stating that the skeleton of a gigantic man, with the head missing, had been unearthed at El Boquin, Nicaragua, in the Chontales district: "The ribs are a yard long and four inches wide and the shin bone is too heavy for one man to carry. 'Chontales' is an Indian word meaning 'wild man.' "

In that same year, on June 9, *The New York Times* published a story about the discovery of giant human skeletons. According to the account, three fishermen had found the skeletal remains of humans eight feet tall in the sand of an uninhabited little island off Southern Florida.

Commenting on a fragment of one of the skulls, E.M. Miller, a zoologist at the University of Miami, said the mandible was that of a man and was probably several hundred years old. The fishermen stated that the skulls were unusually thick, the jaws protruded, and the eye sockets were high in the head.

* * *

Certain researchers have suggested that these strange humanoid skeletal remains may not be the bones of huge members of *Homo sapiens*, but of some related species, such as the creatures known as "The Abominable Snowman," the "Wildman of China," "Bigfoot," "Sasquatch," or "Yeti." These creatures are usually described as nearly seven feet tall, five hundred to six hundred pounds, and covered with reddish hair. After years of scoffing at sightings of giant manlike beasts from California to China, many serious scientists are beginning to consider that they might well have been wrong in dismissing the reports of "Sasquatch" as *tall* tales.

In May, 1990, Frank Poirier of Ohio State University released the results of an analysis of hair samples left by China's famous "Wildman." The hair proved to be neither human nor ape, but more closely matched human hair. The analysis indicated a "high likelihood of the existence of these creatures."

Poirier explained that Chinese legends of the wildmen went back as much as 3,000 years, and in his opinion, may be accounts of creatures descended from a type of giant ape extinct for 400,000 years.

"As a scientist, I'm embarrassed to say it," Poirier admitted. "We were so sure these things didn't exist."

4
The Mystery
of Lost Civilizations

Who constructed the serpentine temple in Brittany
that winds along for 8 miles and contains more than
10,000 massive stones, 300 of which are over 15 feet
tall?

What physical — or mental — giants built the
pre-Incan Andean fortress of Sacsahuaman? How
were primitive Peruvians able to hoist several
hundred stone blocks, some of which weigh over
two hundred tons, more than two miles above sea
level?

Whose features inspired the gigantic stone faces
twelve to thirty feet tall scattered about Easter
Island in the South Pacific?

What forgotten peoples created Baalbeck plat-
forms in ancient Syria? How were they able to raise
stone slabs weighing 1,200 tons to the top of 54
pillars that reach more than 90 feet into the desert
air?

Or what about India's famous Black Pagoda? The

temple stands 228 feet high and supports a single stone slab that is estimated at a weight of 2,000 tons. Could even the most powerful modern derrick hoist a 2,000-ton bulk without collapsing under the massive burden?

In the African nation of Zimbabwe lies an ancient temple constructed of more than one million six- by six- by twelve-inch granite blocks. What is so startling is that absolutely no granite exists within hundreds of miles. How did the ancient people manage to transport over one million granite blocks for such great distances?

In 1965, Professor Dragoslav Srejovec of the University of Belgrade, Yugoslavia, excavated remains indicating that civilization existed in the Balkans at the same time that primitive villages were being built in the Middle East. Massive stone faces that may have represented household gods were dug up along the banks of the Danube River about sixty miles from Belgrade. Further excavation later produced the remains of a town that, according to radiocarbon dating techniques, dated back to approximately 7000 B.C.

Has civilization on Earth been cyclical? Has mankind reached heights of technology that may be even greater than our own — only to pass away to dust and then begin all over again? Or have "gods" from spaceships descended from time to time to help early humans build some of those truly "impossible" structures?

The 885-foot Wall
on Fort Mountain, Georgia

Cherokee Indians, ancient Welshmen, and a vanished civilization of blond sun-worshippers have, at various times, been credited with the building of the 885-foot wall on Fort Mountain in northern Georgia. The wall runs from east to west and looms over twenty-nine pits that look as if they might have served as ancient "foxholes" from which defenders fought against invaders. The wall ranges from a height of seven feet to only two or three feet. The large amount of rubble along the wall suggests that at one time it might have been much higher.

Who Laid the Beautiful Mosaic Tile
in Oklahoma City?

On June 27, 1969, workmen leveling a rock shelf at 122nd Street on the Broadway Extension between Edmond and Oklahoma City, Oklahoma, uncovered what appeared to be an inlaid mosaic tile floor that covered several thousand square feet.

"I'm sure this was man-made because the stones are placed in perfect sets of parallel lines which intersect to form a diamond shape, all pointing to the east," said Durwood Pate, a geologist who studied the site. "We found post holes which measure a perfect two rods from the other two. The top of the stone is very smooth, and if you lift one of them, you will find it is very jagged, which indicates wear on the surface. Everything is too well placed to be a natural formation."

Delbert Smith, a geologist, president of the Oklahoma Seismograph Company, agreed that the mosaic tile had been laid there, but by whom?

The Great Stone Walls
of an Ancient Fort in Texas

In Rockwall, Texas's smallest county, there are four great stone walls of an ancient fort running for four square miles, some portions of which are eight inches thick and reach heights of fifty feet. The stones have been placed on top of each other with the ends breaking near the center of the stone above or below, just as a fine mason would construct a wall. The stones give the appearance of having been beveled around their edges, and some of the larger ones have been inscribed with some form of writing. Archaeologists have said that the walled "city" is remarkably similar in appearance to cities excavated in North Africa and the Middle East.

Mystery Monoliths in New England

On September 6, 1969, James P. Whittall, Jr., an archaeologist for the New England Antiquities Research Association, announced that radiocarbon testing of some strange stone structures in New England proved that they had been built about 3,000 years ago. Artifacts found in stone chambers near the structures suggested that they had been built by a culture similar to those living in the Mediterranean from about 3000 B.C. to 500 B.C.

Whittall's theory is that the stonework is very similar to structures of a culture known to have inhabited the Iberian [Spanish] peninsula. Other experts believe the work may be of Phoenician origin. A number of archaeologists have long theorized that certain Bronze age explorers may have successfully challenged the Atlantic and found their way to America.

Coins from Long-forgotten Mints

In addition to mysterious structures, a number of really unusual metal coins has been unearthed in North America.

During September, 1833, workmen boring for water near Norfolk, Virginia, found a coin that experts declared was stamped with figures representing a "warrior or hunter and other characters, apparently of Roman origin."

Jacob W. Moffit, of Chillicothe, Illinois, brought up a coin while drilling at a depth of 120 feet. It appeared to be some kind of astrological talisman with the signs of Pisces and Leo and a legend inscribed upon it in a language, according to a linguistics expert, "somewhere between Arabic and Phoenician without being either."

North American Mining Activity in Prehistory

What forgotten people worked the copper mines of Lake Superior? Extensive mines have been found that were obviously worked by a highly skilled people. The local Indian tribes, however, have absolutely no tradition relating to these mines; and not a single artifact or bit of bone has ever been found to reveal the identity of these prehistoric miners.

Could they have been the source for the mysterious copper coins that keep turning up around the United States?

In May, 1953, workers of the Lion Coal Cops Wattis mine of Wattis, Utah, broke into a vast network of tunnels that appeared to be very old. Pockets of coal within these strange tunnels had oxidized to the stage where coal could nearly be scooped with the bare hands. The miners also reported finding rooms where the coal had been processed.

What is thought to be the oldest of all lost mines in North America was found in 1961 in the Mojave Desert, southeast of Twenty-Nine Palms, California. Barry Storm, the discoverer, states that highly skilled prehistoric Mayans worked the site for jade when the desert country was a series of lush valleys. Radiocarbon testings indicate that the mine was in operation around 1500 B.C.

The "City of the Dead" Was an Ancient Ruin Before the Incas Arrived in Peru

When the Incas were a flourishing empire, the remains of a city they named Tiahuanaco, the "city of the dead," were ancient ruins. Bits of pottery and other artifacts indicate that the city may be 20,000 years old, and that its unknown inhabitants may have created a culture in prehistoric Bolivia that was remarkably advanced.

From what little evidence is available for study, experts have determined that the inhabitants of Tiahuanaco were a much taller people than the present dwellers of the high plateau. And they did not have the prominent cheekbones generally associated with the American Indian of the region.

In 1964, Professor Frederic Engel and his associates discovered the ruins of a city in Peru at least 9,000 years old. When they unearthed the skeletal remains of the former inhabitants, they discovered that these people, too, were taller than the present tribes of the area. Exactly who these people were is still a mystery.

In 1966, Dr. Robert J. Menzies located the remains of an ancient city 6,000 feet beneath the surface of the ocean off the coast of Lima, Peru. Old Inca ruins dot the nearby shore, and archaeologists are convinced that the remains of even older civilizations are certain to be found as time goes on. But a city that lies 6,000 feet under the sea could, indeed, lead to what Dr. Menzies speculated as "one of the most exciting discoveries of this century."

Will the Dig at Tucume Link Meso-America to Egypt and Atlantis?

Norwegian explorer Thor Heyerdahl believes that the ancient pre-Inca culture that created pyramid structures in Peru may provide the missing link in a virtual chain of civilizations that connect Meso-America to Egypt, Mesopotamia, the Indus Valley, and possibly the lost continent of Atlantis. Early in 1990, Heyerdahl announced that he had agreed to organize the archaeological dig at the site of Tucume, a newly discovered center of an advanced pre-Inca civilization.

In describing why, at the age of 75, he would

seek to undertake such a task, Heyerdahl replied in the April 2, 1990, issue of *U.S. News and World Report:*

"When I first came through the . . . trees that hide the view to the ruins, I felt as if I were dreaming. I had never seen anything like this before. Eroded by the centuries, these pyramids have never been damaged by looters nor excavated by archaeologists . . . There were mummy masks and royal paraphernalia of gold inlaid with lapis lazuli, green turquoise and tropical spondylus shells. None of these materials exist in Peru. . . . The early art of these pyramid builders shows that they built large ships of reed bundles . . . with such vessels they must have sailed all the way down the South American coast. . . ."

The Enigma of the Great Mayan Roads

One of the great mysteries of South American archaeological and anthropological studies is why the Mayans, who were ignorant of the wheel and had no vehicles or carts, built some of the broadest highways in the world. One extraordinary boulevard is said to be wide enough to park eight modern automobiles side by side. These avenues, which are made of limestone blocks and surfaced with limestone cement, stretch out for miles across mountains and jungles.

The Remarkable Accuracy
of Mayan Astronomy

The paradox of great highways for a people without wheels is all the more baffling when one considers the precision of Mayan astronomical knowledge. An inscription on the wall of the tomb in the Pyramid at Palenque speaks of a month of 29.53086 days. The Mayans at Copan estimated the lunar month as a bit less than 29.53020 days. Contemporary astronomical measurement states that the correct figure is found in the average between these two calculations.

The Mayans estimated the earthly year at 365.2420 days. Modern science has bettered the estimate by only 2 one-hundred-thousandths of a day.

The Mayans were aware of the number of years and days it takes Jupiter to circle once around the zodiac. They knew that Mars became a brilliant midnight star every 780 days. They calculated the length of Venus's year and recognized the pattern of days that Venus appears as an evening star — as well as the fact that the pattern is repeated every eight years.

The first astronomical conference on the North American continent took place 1,400 years ago in the ancient Mayan city of Copan, located deep in the jungles of what is now Honduras. This noteworthy occasion was commemorated in an elaborately carved altarpiece, with representations on its side of the sixteen scientists in attendance.

Misplaced Mummies

Everyone knows that the Egyptians preserved their dead, but no one knows who prepared the mummies found in eastern Sonora State, Mexico. Thirty mummies, perfectly preserved, dressed in rich clothing and lavish jewelry, obviously of the priesthood — all more than 10,000 years old — were found resting in a large cave sealed with a huge boulder. No clues were found to suggest what lost Mexican civilization might have preserved the bodies of their dead in the manner of the Egyptians.

A Female Mummy over Seven Feet Tall Found in California

In July, 1895, a party of miners was working near Bridlevale Falls, California. G.F. Martindale, who was in charge, noticed a pile of stones placed against the wall of a cliff in an unnatural formation. Assuming the rocks had been stacked by human hands, Martindale told his men to begin removing the stones to investigate what might lie inside.

The miners were astonished when they found a wall of rock that had been shaped and fitted together with an apparent knowledge of masonry. The joints between the blocks were all of a uniform eighth-of-an-inch thickness.

The men became excited, believing they had stumbled upon some lost treasure trove, and eagerly began tearing down the wall.

Instead of riches, however, the miners found a large mummified corpse lying on a ledge that had been carved from natural stone. The men lighted their carbide head lamps and tried to transform their disappointment into a more profitable search of the burial vault. But all the chamber contained was the mummy of a very large woman that had been wrapped in animal skins and covered with a fine gray powder. A closer examination revealed that she clutched a child to her breast.

When the mummy was taken to Los Angeles, scientists there agreed that the woman had been the citizen of a race that had lived on the North American continent long before American Indians had become dominant. They further arrived at a consensus that the skeleton's height of six feet eight inches would have represented a height in life of at least seven feet. Figuring the classic height difference between men and women, they supposed that some males of the forgotten species might have stood nearly eight feet tall.

Found: A Maternity Ward for Giants

On July 30, 1974, the *Dallas Morning News* carried the story of the discovery of skeletal remains of a seven-foot woman sealed in a cave near the Texas town of Chalk Mountain. The astonishing find was made by Dr. Ernest Adams, an attorney and amateur archaeologist. It was Dr. Adams's theory that the woman was of average size for her unknown race, and that "the cave was a maternity ward for such giants . . . The cave was steam-heated by water boiled under the floor . . . [she] died in childbirth apparently. And her perfect teeth suggested that she was quite young."

The Mystery of
Costa Rica's Large Round Stones

While some undetermined culture was busy making mummies in Mexico and North America, another mysterious lost people was industriously shaping large stone spheres in the hot tropical forests of Costa Rica. Some of the weird balls weigh only a few pounds, but others are as large as eight feet in diameter and weigh more than sixteen tons. Archaeologists have excavated under the balls, seeking hidden burial places, but have found nothing.

Some of the strange balls are arranged in rows, others in circles, still others in triangles. Certain researchers have suggested that they may have been used for religious purposes or in an attempt to chart the stars, but at this moment no one knows for certain.

Petroglyphs of Great Reptiles
and Large Pointy-Nosed Humanoids

On the subject of mysterious stones, Dr. Javier Cabrera of Ica, Peru, has a collection of more than 15,000 engraved stones that appear to depict a very unusual race of humanoids living side by side with the great prehistoric reptiles.

Dr. Cabrera's stones range in size from fist-sized to boulders, but they are all covered with weird carvings. Many of the largest depict bizarre, pointy-nosed people with five fingers and no thumbs, fighting off dinosaurs with Viking-styled battle-axes.

Dr. Cabrera is a medical doctor who specializes in circulatory ailments by day and conducts archaeological digs by night. He claims that he began finding the mysterious rocks near Ica more than twenty years ago after an earthquake provoked a landslide that exposed a large deposit of the picture rocks. Many who don't believe him insist that Cabrera hires Indians to carve the stones. To the frustration of those who defend him, Cabrera refuses to divulge the exact location of the mysterious cache of stones so that impartial experts might examine the site for themselves. Dr. Cabrera holds fast to his theory that the carvings were done by people who lived near Ica from 250,000 to one million years ago.

Some of the most remarkable engravings appear to depict the strange five-fingered people conducting brain surgeries, heart transplants, liver operations, and other medical procedures that have no known counterparts. Others show them riding horses and pulling wheeled carts and other vehicles.

Strangely enough, all of the carvings depict people without opposing thumbs. Because even the most primitive apes have opposing thumbs, Dr. Cabrera sees this as additional proof that these people predated the apes. He also asserts that the prehistoric humanoids were destroyed by a cataclysmic disaster after accomplishing many important contributions to the future, including the pyramids of Egypt.

If the Cabrera stones should ever be authenticated, then all of our accepted theories about human genesis will be turned inside out. Our species may not only have existed millions of years earlier than we ever imagined, but a strange, five-fingered, pointy-nosed species of humanoids may have lived at the time of the dinosaurs.

How little we know of the past — and how very much the past might be able to tell us about our future.

5
The Perplexing Enigma
of Vanishing Islands

Sarah Ann Island, located just north of the equator, had been noted by astronomers as being directly in the path of a total solar eclipse scheduled for June 8, 1937. Scientists were eager to set up an observation post on the island, as there were no others in the vicinity.

The U.S. Pacific Fleet set out in the summer of 1937 in search of the island; but both they and the astronomers were disappointed. Sarah Ann Island had vanished and has never been located again.

How could an entire island, charted on all the sea maps, vanish? No one knows the answer to that question, but Sarah Ann is not alone in her bizarre disappearing act.

Imagine how perplexed Captains Cornwallis and Horsburgh, two experienced seamen, must have been when, at different times, they each sailed over an area in the South Atlantic in a vain search for the charted site of Saxemberg Island.

The island had been discovered by Dutch navigator Lindeman in 1670. In 1804, Captain Galloway of the American schooner *Fanny* described the island as low-lying and supporting a high-peaked hill in its center. He reported that he had the island in view for four hours.

The island was seen again in 1816 by Captain Head of the British *True Briton*. Captain Head and his crew had Saxemberg Island in their sights for a total of six hours. He, too, remarked on the peaked hill in the middle of the landmass.

But when Captain Cornwallis approached the area in 1821 there was no Saxemberg to be seen. Several years later, Captain Horsburgh explored the same area of sea and was equally dumbfounded by his inability to locate the island. To add to the confusion, the persistent Horsburgh took soundings at the location that revealed a depth of 2,000 fathoms (12,000 feet).

What happened to Sarah Ann and Saxemberg Islands? Both were sighted by more than one ocean-going vessel. Both were geographically located on all official charts and maps. There was so little reason to doubt the existence of Sarah Ann that astronomers were planning to build an observation post on it. Yet subsequent voyages to these phantom islands failed to locate them.

These two are not the only cases of islands that have been mysteriously lost. The phenomenon of vanishing islands has been with us for centuries. How is it possible for an island to simply disappear?

One theory focuses on the fact that the Pacific Ocean bed, which happens to be the location of more vanishing islands than any other, is extremely unstable. The floor of the ocean contains many faults and is the scene of frequent volcanic eruptions. Islands are often formed by these volcanic thrusts, some of them issuing from depths of 16,000 feet.

With such unstable origins, and formed primarily of porous volcanic material, these islands — "children of the volcano" — are completely at the mercy of wind and wave erosion. Perhaps the sea swallows the islands up just as simply as it spews them out in the first place.

Urania Island is a good illustration of this instability. In February, 1946, approximately two hundred miles south of Tokyo, a British warship observed the origin of two landmasses and noted that the cones reached a height of fifty feet. The islands occupied the space of about one square mile. It was decided that the two cones represented one landmass, and the British Admiralty christened it Urania Island, after the vessel that had discovered it.

Scarcely two months later, however, Urania Island had degenerated to a shoal occupying a considerably larger area.

It is precisely this kind of appearing-and-disappearing act that has confounded mapmakers and geographers for decades, causing them to place, then remove, islands from their maps.

The Vanishing Aurora Islands

Another set of mystery islands met with such a fate when they were discovered early in the 1760s by the sailing ship *Aurora*. The captain marked their location somewhere southeast of the Falklands and named them the Auroras.

After the initial sighting, the islands were seen by several other vessels and were eventually surveyed by a Danish ship especially equipped for the task. The position of the Auroras was entered on all official maps, and they would have remained there had it not been for a certain captain who was sailing through the area and decided to make a visit.

The captain carefully plotted his course, and in due time arrived at the place marked AURORAS on his map. But there were no islands. The captain searched the area in astonishment — until he was forced to conclude that the Auroras had vanished.

Further searches for the lost islands were conducted in 1820 and 1822. In a matter of a few years, numerous vessels had explored the area. But no clue to the disappearance of the Auroras has ever been discovered. Seen by so many ships before they vanished, the islands must have existed at one time. So where did they go?

Playing Cat and Mouse with Bouvet Island

In 1739, Antarctic explorer Pierre des Loziers Bouvet discovered an island approximately 1,500 miles from the Cape of Good Hope, which he described as being five miles in diameter and partially covered by a glacier.

After its discovery, Bouvet Island played cat and mouse with Captain James Cook in 1772 and in 1775, and with Captain Furneaux in 1774, neither of whom was able to locate it. The island's very existence was questioned until 1808, when two sealing vessels, the *Snow Swan* and the *Otter*, both reported having seen it. All doubts were erased in 1822 when Captain Benjamin Morrell claimed to have landed upon the island and killed a number of seals.

In 1825, two whaling vessels visited Bouvet. One of these was the *Sprightly* whose skipper Captain George Norris sighted additional landmasses. Captain Norris sailed all the way around an island he called Thompson, and he noted three rocky islets that he named the Chimneys. All four of the newly discovered islands were located forty-five miles northeast of Bouvet.

For a time the islands were recorded on all the admiralty charts, until two expeditions — one in 1843 and another in 1845 — failed to find any sign of them. The captains of the expeditionary ships agreed that the previous explorers had been deceived by "phantom" islands, and the landmasses were removed from the official charts and maps.

But Bouvet Island refused to be so easily dismissed. In the following decades it was sighted by three different vessels. The captain of one ship even made several sketches of it. Confusion reigned. When Bouvet Island was on the maps, it was not to be found. When it was removed, sea captains kept bumping into it.

Finally, in 1898, the German ship *Valdivia* definitely found Bouvet Island — exactly where Pierre Bouvet had said it was 154 years earlier. The *Valdivia* was unable to locate Captain Norris's Thompson Island or the Chimneys, however, leaving their existence still under the shadow of doubt.

Within a very short period of time, three more ships positioned Bouvet Island, and as of 1917, it has officially existed and is marked on all charts and maps. Thompson Island and the Chimneys, which Norris plotted as being forty-five miles north-northeast of Bouvet, remain unaccounted for to this day. Perhaps they, too, will be rediscovered in the future, and will be found to occupy the very place allotted to them by Captain Norris.

The Mystery of St. Juan de Lisboa

The island of St. Juan de Lisboa is supposedly located in the southern Indian Ocean. For a century and a half this independent little island managed to elude the government of France in its efforts to add it to their possessions. To this day, the island remains a puzzle to geographers.

The first mention of St. Juan de Lisboa came from M. de la Roche Saint André, who was sent to Madagascar in 1655. Using a Portuguese map of the area, he searched for the island, but was unable to locate it. Because of his failure to find the landmass, people quickly lost interest.

Nearly fifty years later, in 1704, a large number

of men began to include references to the island in their memoirs, providing careful descriptions of its shape and appearance. Such detailed references to the island reignited the French crown's interest in St. Juan de Lisboa.

In 1721, Louis XV ordered the Chevalier de Nyon to take possession of St. Juan in the name of France. But even though the meticulous de Nyon searched the area extensively, he was forced to turn back in disappointment. The island was not to be found.

A few years later, when French Colonial Governor Labourdonnais set sail for his new post, his list of instructions included finding St. Juan and annexing it. After months of frustrated searching, Labourdonnais gave up in total bewilderment.

Although the French government remained convinced that the island truly existed, ships' captains and geographers of the day were beginning to grow extremely doubtful. It was at this point in its long game of hide-and-seek that the wily island decided to spark interest in itself once again.

In 1772, a Monsieur Donjon, second-in-command of the *Bougainville*, jubilantly reported that he had found the island and fixed its precise position. In the midst of a violent storm on April 27, Donjon had sighted St. Juan and had even managed to complete a rough sketch of it.

Hooked once again, the French ordered the Chevalier de Saint Felix of the *Heure du Berger* to hoist anchor immediately and set sail for the spot indicated by Donjon. But in 1773, de Saint Felix confessed his defeat. He simply had been unable to find the island.

In the same year, yet another fruitless attempt was made by the *Etoîle du Matin*, and a few years later, French seaman Kerguelen churned up the sea almost inch by inch, determined to be the one to at last claim the elusive island for France. However, the island apparently was not receiving visitors.

The last French attempt to find St. Juan de Lisboa was made by Advisse des Ruisseaux in 1799. Although he scoured the area for miles around, frustration and defeat eventually overcame him as well.

Shortly thereafter, French power in the Indian Ocean was broken, and the triumphant English made no effort to discover the mysterious island.

Amateur detectives and seasoned seamen have searched for a satisfactory explanation of the mysterious St. Juan de Lisboa. The possibility of human error has largely been dismissed as improbable in this case. Too many expeditions searched too hard and too unrelentingly for the island to have somehow been overlooked.

Nor is it likely that St. Juan was a floating island, a phenomenon most often found in large inland lakes, rather than in salt water oceans. Floating islands rise from beneath the surface of the water and, being unanchored, change position constantly, until they return again to the depths from whence they came. The possibility that St. Juan was a volcanic mass, rising then falling beneath the waves, is a more viable explanation.

The theory most generally accepted today is that the island was invented by Arabian pirates to confuse the Portuguese. By giving "St. Juan de Lisboa" as their place of rendezvous and storehouse for their booty, they could use secluded spots on other islands without fear of attack.

6
Falling Flesh
and Flying Rocks

On October 26, 1956, Mrs. Faye Swanson of Broadmoor, California, stepped out into her backyard at 8:05 A.M. and found the body of a small, furry monkey that had fallen out of the sky during the night. Its little body had struck her clothesline with such violent force that a solid four-by-four post had splintered.

A spokesman from San Francisco International Airport said that no airliner had been transporting monkeys during the night. No authority from any organization could offer an explanation for the source of the fallen monkey, and the *San Francisco Chronicle* headlined the question "Who's Throwing Monkeys at the Earth?"

In the winter of 1955, residents of Senzu-mara, a village on the Japanese island of Oshima, found the carcass of a 5-year-old, 1,000-pound African elephant on their beach. A careful check revealed that no elephants were missing from Japanese zoos, and there were no reports of any elephants having died aboard ship. No serious-minded person would even suggest that the corpse could have drifted intact from Africa to a beach in Japan. As investigators commented, it was as if the huge creature had fallen from the sky.

On August 27, 1968, motorists traveling between Rio de Janeiro and São Paulo in Brazil on the Via Durta Highway were astonished to see a strange rainfall in the distance. It could not be normal rain, the motorists knew, for there were no clouds — and the substance that was falling was much too dark to be ordinary rainwater. When Deputy Marcondes Fereiro arrived on the scene, he found an area of one square kilometer literally strewn with chunks of flesh and blood.

The São Paulo newspapers reported that the pieces of flesh lay approximately two feet apart and varied in size from approximately two to seven inches. The flesh was spongy in texture and violet in color. It had been accompanied by drops of blood.

Authorities were at a loss for an explanation of the strange "sky fall." The weather had been especially clear on that day, and there had been no aircraft reported in the area either before, during, or after the fall — nor were any birds noticed in the vicinity. With no reasonable clue as to the source of the unidentified flesh, the police ended the mysterious affair by destroying all of it.

* * *

In September, 1966, a mysterious lump of "charred material" dropped onto the farm of Carl Retherford near Windfall, Indiana. At first it was thought that the chunk had been part of a huge meteor seen over the Midwest, but subsequent analysis by chemist Michael E. Lipschutz of Purdue University convinced Retherford that the material was "definitely not from a meteor." Retherford himself assured investigators that the chunk could not be a clump of ashes from his own furnace as he did not use coal.

The conclusion? No one knows what it was or how it got there.

Mysterious objects have been falling from the sky for centuries. However, these peculiar rainfalls of flesh, fish, and rocks have always been relegated to the back pages of newspapers and to the forgotten storerooms of museums, largely to be ignored. When these strange sky falls have been considered by conventional scientists, it has been only to dismiss them as oddities.

Around the turn of the century, a journalist named Charles Fort took it upon himself to bring such well-ignored subjects out of the scientific closet. In 1919, he published *The Book of the Damned*, with the note that "By the damned, I mean what science has excluded." The book focused upon a large number of uncomfortable facts that don't appear to fit into the ordinary scheme of things.

Although a growing number of scientists have

been forced to accept the reality of bizarre sky falls, they are having a great deal of difficulty explaining them within the existing scientific structure.

It's Raining Fish in the Desert

On May 3, 1952, Fred H. Koch, a professional photographer whose specialty is taking pictures of lightning, was in the Bingham, New Mexico, area taking pictures of a desert storm. As the winds increased, dirt, dust, and sand began to swirl across the ground and up into the sky. Koch sought refuge in his car, where he waited out nature's rampage.

The afternoon had been very hot, and the soil was dry and parched. Suddenly, the heavens opened up and poured down rain for nearly two hours.

When the sun finally came out again, the photographer left his car and walked out into the desert. Within minutes, the sun was baking the land as mercilessly as before, and the sand had sucked up all the water. With the exception of small puddles of water, it soon appeared as if there had been no rain at all.

As Koch walked along, he was startled to notice that the entire area that he was approaching was covered with hundreds of tiny dead fish. Each of them was about an inch long, and very soft. The slightest pressure crushed them.

Where the puddles of water were larger and deeper, some of the fish were alive and swimming. It was not long, however, before the sun dried up the remaining puddles of water, and the fish died.

Koch was surrounded by the smell of fish, and felt as though he were standing on a beach rather than a desert.

Koch took several photographs of the fish, some of which were published in the local newspaper. The pictures caught the interest of a group of biologists from Lubbock, Texas, who traveled to the area to collect a number of the fish. After studying them, they reported that the fish had prominent eyes and were not related to any of the several species of fish known to inhabit underground pools, so they couldn't have come from a 150-foot well nearby. There were no other lakes, rivers, or ponds within an appreciable distance.

It was not long before a large array of entomologists, biologists, ornithologists, botanists, and archaeologists arrived in the area. There were many theories to explain the fall of the fish, but not one of them seemed to fit the facts. The most logical one was that the storm had drawn up the fish from a large body of water as far north as Colorado. Then as the winds moved south, a low-pressure point developed over the hot, arid desert, causing the heavy clouds to dump their load of fish and water onto a rain belt about two miles wide.

The theory sounded good enough, but Fred Koch did some further investigating and discovered that while the rain belt had been approximately two miles wide where he had been during the storm, it had become much wider a bit farther south. And the fish had only fallen within an area of one square mile. In his opinion, the question remained: How do fish suddenly appear in the middle of a desert?

It's Raining Fish, Salamanders, and Crawfish All Over the Place!

And how did fish suddenly rain down on Pentagon Parkway in Dallas, Texas? Two little girls, Martha Brumley and Barbara Williams, collected about forty in a jar, all about three inches long. The fish, which fell June 18, 1958, were dark gray with reddish-gold spots and red tails.

What caused five-inch-long salamanders to fall in Portal, North Dakota, in October, 1949? Local residents didn't even know what the strange creatures were as they fell from the sky all around them. Many had never before seen a salamander.

In August, 1984, A. D. Ellmers and his wife, Neva, were standing in the driveway of their San Diego home when tiny fish began to fall on them from the sky. Ellmers picked up some of the fish and brought them to an expert who decreed that they *might* be anchovies or little tomcods from the Pacific Ocean. A meteorologist with the National Weather Service released what has become the standard explanation in such cases: An isolated "funnel cloud" sucked up the fish from the ocean and dropped them over San Diego.

And was it the same kind of isolated "funnel cloud" that deposited a crawfish six feet up in a peach tree in Eberton, Georgia? Or dropped a goldfish down Mrs. Walker's chimney in Whitechurch, Bristol, England?

Chunks of Ice That Fall from the Sky

By far the most common of the mysterious objects to fall from the sky are large chunks of ice. Even stranger, the icefalls seem to have almost deliberate aim.

On March 11, 1966, a block of ice weighing between twenty-five and thirty pounds sailed through the air at an angle and smashed to a resounding halt atop a parked car belonging to Frank Haynes. Fortunately, he was lunching at a nearby restaurant when the impact occurred.

On March 26, 1966, Mrs. Lorraine Nuckels of San Mateo, California, sat watching television with her family when they suddenly heard something that sounded like a bomb exploding in their house. An ice chunk measuring about one square foot had hurtled through their roof and missed them by about fifteen feet. In addition, ice chips the size of baseballs circled the house in a 150-foot perimeter.

Although the icefalls are most commonly blamed on aircraft passing overhead, the aviation industry claims that no known icing conditions would cause huge ice bombs to drop on unsuspecting people below. Also, in the two cases above, there were no airplanes seen or heard over the area either before or at the time the ice crashed through the roof or cartop.

But if the icefalls do not come from planes flying overhead, where do they come from? Outer space? UFOs?

You would especially want to know the answer to that question if you were Ronald Phipps, and a chunk of ice weighing several pounds put a hole in your roof.

Or if you were a passerby on Arch Street, in Brownsville, Pennsylvania, when a hunk of ice weighing about twenty-five pounds crashed to the sidewalk directly in front of you.

Or if you were Dominick Bacigalupo of Madison Township, New Jersey, and a seventy-pound cake of ice exploded through your roof, totally demolishing two kitchen chairs.

Falling Mathematical Formulae over Albany, New York

At 4:15 P.M. on July 24, 1973, Bob Hill, owner of radio station WHRL in North Greenbush (Albany), New York, was taking out the station's garbage when a tiny twinkle in the sky caught his eye. The station's tower is three hundred feet high, and the twirling specks Hill saw were falling from a much greater distance.

Hill went into the station, grabbed his $20 \times$ binoculars, and tried to focus on the drifting objects. "I'm certain that the things must have been above 10,000 feet," he recalled. "The sky was crystal clear. There was nothing to interfere with my observation. It took something like half an hour to 45 minutes for the objects to land."

Hill got into his car and drove down Lape Road. There he saw two of the white objects land in a hayfield. He ran out into the field to find "two sets of formulae and accompanying graphs that explain 'normalized extinction' and the mysterious 'incomplete David-Greenstein orientation.' "

The cryptic mathematical formulae lay scattered around a very puzzled Bob Hill. "The thing that really bugged me," he complained, "was that there was nothing on the papers that would identify them as belonging to anybody. You know, if it were a thesis or a manuscript, there would have been some identification. If the sheets belonged to a government project, they would have been stamped all over."

Hill did learn that the formulae actually dealt with a known physical process. "You first think of something kind of ominous when you read about 'normalized extinction,' but I checked with three Ph.D.s and a friend of mine who is a nuclear physicist, and they recognized the data. It has something to do with light out of phase with itself, light canceling itself out. It is actual research data."

But what was it doing falling out of nowhere onto a hayfield outside of Albany?

Hill made inquiries at the Federal Aviation Administration, the National Weather Service, the FBI, and the Albany Airport Control Tower, but no one could provide him with *any* clues about the mysterious falling formulae.

"Those papers fell out of a brilliant, dark blue sky," Hill said, remaining insistent about what he had perceived. "There was not a cloud in sight. I would have been able to see any aircraft. Only an upper-atmospheric weather balloon would have been so high that I would not have been able to see it. I checked, and there was no upper-atmospheric research being conducted. Those formulae just dropped out of the sky, and I would certainly like to know where they came from!"

Who Dumped Sahara Sand over Southern and Central England?

Authorities in Great Britain were able to identify the nearly two tons of sand per square mile that were dumped over southern and central England sometime during the night of June 30, 1968, as having come from the Sahara Desert. Angry and confused Britons stepped outside on the morning of July 1 to discover that their houses, lawns, and cars had been splattered with a layer of red, yellow, or brown dust and sprinkled with sand. A freak storm, the meteorologists announced in the official response, had brought the awful mess from the Sahara Desert, thousands of miles away across a mighty ocean.

But Ronald J. Willis, a devotee of the works of Charles Fort, master collector of stories such as these, pointed out that no one had bothered to find other records of the " . . . fantastic storm that had picked up several million tons of the Sahara and toted it over populated North Africa, maybe France and Spain, and dropped its load over jolly old England. There are no reports of any such red rain in any other European country at that time."

Weird Things Keep Falling from Our Skies

Stranger things have fallen from the skies. Charles Fort reported the following sky falls:

August 20, 1870: Large crystals of salt fell in Switzerland.

Winter, 1876: Worms, which could only have fallen from the sky, were found crawling over the frozen snow in Christiania, Norway.

July 3, 1886: Hordes of land snails fell near Redruth, England, during a heavy thunderstorm. The snails, reported as "quite different from any previously known in the district," were so numerous that they could be gathered by the hatful.

July 3, 1860: The sidewalks of Montreal, Quebec, were covered with lizards that had dropped from the sky.

But not every mysterious sky fall drops something unpleasant. On the evening of May 16, 1965, Stanley Morris of Louisville, Kentucky, heard a noise so loud that he jumped from his chair. Concerned, he stepped outside to his backyard and found the roof of his garage covered with bags of cookies. He quickly realized that his neighbors on either side had also been blessed with the goodies. There were no identifying marks on any of the bags. Cookies from Heaven!

7
People Who Walk
into the Past

On October 23, 1963, Mrs. Coleen Buterbaugh of Lincoln, Nebraska, was walking across the campus of Nebraska Wesleyan where she was a secretary to Dr. Sam Dahl, Dean of the college. At exactly 8:50 A.M., she entered the old C.C. White Building, which was used primarily as a music hall.

Her heels clicked softly as she walked down the long corridor to an office at the end. She could hear the sound of a marimba being played by a practicing musician. Yawning, whispering students were leaving their first-hour classes for either another classroom or a welcome cup of coffee. Just before Mrs. Buterbaugh entered the office of Dr. Tom McCourt, a visiting lecturer from Scotland, she mused to herself that it was a typical early morning scene at Nebraska Wesleyan.

But what waited for Coleen Buterbaugh in Dr. McCourt's office was far from typical.

As she stepped into the two-room suite, Mrs.

Buterbaugh was struck by an almost overwhelming odor of musty air. When she had first opened the door to the office, she had observed that both rooms were empty and that the windows were open. But at that moment . . .

"I had the strange feeling that I was not alone in the office," she later told Rose Sipe of the Lincoln *Evening Journal*. "I looked up, and for what must have been just a few seconds, saw the figure of a woman, standing with her back to me, at a cabinet in the second office. She was reaching up into one of the drawers."

Mrs. Buterbaugh could no longer hear the noisy babble of the students in the outer hall as they passed to and from their classes. She had the eerie feeling that she had suddenly become isolated from reality.

The "other secretary," who seemed to be filing cards so industriously, was tall, slender, and dark-haired. Her clothing was definitely of another period — a long-sleeved, white shirtwaist, and an ankle-length brown skirt.

"I felt the presence of a man sitting at the desk to my left," Mrs. Buterbaugh told Ms. Sipe. "But as I turned around, there was no one there.

"I gazed out the large window behind the desk, and the scenery seemed to be that of many years ago. There were no streets. The new Williard sorority house that now stands across the lawn was not there: Nothing outside was modern.

"By then I was frightened, so I turned and left the room!"

As Mrs. Buterbaugh hurried back to her desk in Dean Dahl's office, she kept trying to convince herself that her imagination had been playing tricks on her. She sat down at her typewriter and tried to work on the letters that the Dean had dictated. It was no good. Her nervous, shaky fingers refused to obey. She had to tell someone about her experience. It was too much to keep to herself.

When she entered the Dean's office, he rose to his feet and helped her to a chair, for she seemed so pale and shaken. He listened to her story, and then, without mocking her, asked her to accompany him to the office of Dr. Glenn Callan, chairman of the division of social sciences, who had been on the Wesleyan faculty since 1900. Once again, Mrs. Buterbaugh was fortunate enough to have a listener who heard her out and treated her experience with respect.

After carefully quizzing Mrs. Buterbaugh and piecing together a number of clues from her strange tale, Dr. Callan concluded that the secretary had somehow managed to "walk" into the office as it had been at some time in the 1920s. The woman who she had seen had undoubtedly been Miss Clara Mills, whose office it was at that time. Miss Mills had come to Wesleyan as head of the music theory department and as instructor in piano and music appreciation. The music teacher had been found dead in her office one morning in the late 1930s.

Although Mrs. Buterbaugh's experience was quite startling, her encounter with the past was really rather calm compared to what some others have experienced.

Restored Scenes of Famous Battles

In England, in 1642, a few months after the famous Battle of Edgehill, it was reported that the battle was mysteriously being fought again. King Charles II sent three of his most trusted officers to investigate. The officers watched the phantom battle on two consecutive nights and even recognized several of their comrades who had been killed only a few months before.

On August 4, 1951, two young Englishwomen vacationing in Dieppe, France, were awakened before dawn by the sounds of shellfire, divebombing, and the scraping of landing craft hitting the beach. Nine years before, nearly a thousand young Canadians had been slaughtered in World War II's ill-fated Dieppe raid. The record that the Englishwomen kept of the times and events of the battle was *identical to the minute* with accounts of the raid kept in the British War Office.

Terrified woodcutters and soldiers have reported coming face to face with the images of men fighting and dying on the small island of Corregidor in the Philippines, where in the early days of World War II, a handful of American and Filipino troops fought in vain to halt the Japanese advance.

Visiting an English Country Fair

On a rainy night in October, 1916, Miss Edith Oliver drove off the main road and traveled up a long stone avenue near Avebury, England. She spent some time observing laughing townsfolk at a village fair walking merrily about, then she resumed her drive.

It was not until nine years later that Miss Oliver revisited Avebury. At this time, she learned not only that village fairs had been abolished in *1850*, but that the particular avenue on which she had driven had disappeared before *1800*!

A Search for a Lovely Street
That Disappeared

A few years ago, Russell Kirk told an interesting story to the *Los Angeles Times*. Mr. Kirk was exploring the ancient city of York, England, one night, in order to kill some time between trains. As he was rushing back to the station, he happened to glance down a short street lined with beautiful seventeenth- and eighteenth-century houses. The dimly lighted street looked as enchanting as a scene from a fairy tale.

But Kirk had to catch a train, and he had no time to stop, however much he might have liked to spend hours wandering along the picturesque street. He made himself a promise to return to York in a few months and take a long leisurely stroll down the interesting street.

Kirk stated that he went back to York at least once a year for more than ten years. He vowed that he became thoroughly familiar with every street and lane and practically every house in York — but he was never again to discover the quaint, beautiful little street. Once, however, in a deteriorated section of York, he did find the remains of a formerly elegant street that resembled the one he had glimpsed on that strange night. The quarter is called St. Saviourgate, and a clergyman told Kirk that the section had been desolate since around 1914.

Kirk admitted that he had often wondered what might have happened if he had decided to miss his London train that night, and had wandered into the street. What might have occurred if he had stopped to knock at one of the delightful houses? Would he have stepped into another dimension of time and closed the door upon his own era?

Witnessing a Sacred Seneca Ceremony from Long Ago

When the Bercels built their new home in Ebenezer, New York, they understood that the lot had originally been part of the Seneca Indian Reservation. On the night of February 22, 1966, Carolyn Bercel went for a walk with her dog along the Cazenovia Creek. From out of nowhere came the howl of a strange dog. Her own dog froze, his ears pricked, his tail high, his hackles rising.

Then on the creek bank a tall pole appeared, decorated with cloth strips in vivid colors. As Carolyn watched in astonishment, a buckskin-clad Indian wearing a strange headdress began to strangle a beautiful white dog.

"After he had killed the dog, he wrapped its limp body in bright-colored strips of cloth," she said later. "Next he wound strands of wampum about the animal's broken neck. Dimly I discerned glowing campfires and throbbing drums, and the smell of tobacco smoke penetrated my nostrils."

Soon the scene faded, and Carolyn Bercel stood there shivering in the snow, her own dog whimpering, leaning fearfully against her leg. Later she learned that what she had witnessed was the Seneca Indian's New Year Jubilee ceremony, in which a pure white dog was sacrificed for the sins of the tribe. But her research indicated that the last time the ceremony had taken place on those grounds was in 1841. Had time somehow turned backward for Carolyn Bercel?

Encountering a Wagon Train from Frontier Days

As an author of many books dealing with mysterious occurrences, I receive a great deal of mail from readers around the world. Not long ago, one of my readers, who drives a rig across the western and midwestern plains for a big commercial trucking company, wrote to tell me of a very strange experience. Late one night, while driving his truck, he came upon what appeared to be a wagon train from frontier days.

"I've been teased unmercifully about this story, but I know what I saw: Teams of oxen tugging at heavy Conestoga wagons. Men, women, kids, trudging along behind or beside the big wagons. Dogs trotting and nipping at the heels of the horses ridden by a few armed men.

"Some of the guys have said that maybe it was some folks celebrating a centennial or something historical, but I've seen things like that, and they usually use tractors or horses to pull old wagons — and there is a whole different look about modern people pretending to be long-ago people.

"Others have asked that if it really was a wagon train from out of the past, why were they traveling at night? Why weren't they camped in a circle, like in the old John Wayne movies?

"I don't know, maybe because it was some kind of forced march or something. The people all looked really tired and dead beat. Yes, I could see their faces in the moonlight. It was all that clear.

"I had the feeling that if I had stopped, I could have heard the creaking of harnesses and the squeaking of those big wheels. I did slow way down beside them, but I felt it was all too spooky to stop the truck. While some drivers tease me about my experience, a lot of others have told me that they, too, have seen some really weird things on late night runs across the plains."

Camping with Spanish *Conquistadores*

On a pleasant weekend in August, 1941, Leonard Hall and a number of friends were camping on the upper Current River in the Ozarks. Sometime before dawn, Hall was awakened by the sound of strange voices.

Startled, he opened his eyes to see several figures moving around a roaring fire about one hundred yards from his tent. As he looked about him, he was even more amazed to see that the clearing on the beach was ringed by a dozen campfires.

Most of the shadowy figures seemed to be American Indians, naked except for breech clouts. Hall heard the occasional stamp of a horse's hoof, the murmur of voices speaking in several alien tongues. Some of the language sounded like Spanish, and Hall blinked his eyes in wonder as he noticed that a number of the men seated around the campfires wore the rusted armor of Spanish *conquistadores* from the sixteenth century.

Hall convinced himself that he was either having a wild dream or else he was losing his mind. He didn't want to awaken his companions and have them think he was crazy, so he crawled back into his bedroll and managed to fall asleep.

When he awoke the next morning and found no trace of the phantom campers, Hall did not bother to tell his friends about his bizarre "dream." Nevertheless, he remained curious about his strange experience and decided to do a bit of research.

The "bit" of research became rather extensive, and it was not until many years later — in 1956 — that he gave his eerie story to the St. Louis *Post-Dispatch*. His studies had disclosed the fact that in August, 1541, bands of *conquistadores* under the leadership of De Soto and Coronado had actually been in the Ozark area of the Current River.

Could it be that exactly four hundred years later, Hall and his friends had camped on the very ground where a party of gold-seeking Spaniards and their Indian guides had built their own campfires? How was Leonard Hall able to perceive flames reflecting off tarnished armor *four centuries later*?

He Drove into the Past on His Way Home from Work

Here is a report sent to me from a man, living in a large city on the east coast of the United States, who appears to have driven into the past on his way home from work one night:

"I was driving along the regular route that I took to and from my job at the mill when all of a sudden I didn't recognize the buildings around me. I thought, 'Hey, have I taken a wrong turn?' But I've lived in this city for years now, and I know it pretty darn well. I don't see how I could have taken a wrong turn on a route that I drive twice a day, six days a week. And, no, I had not been drinking. And I don't do drugs.

"Everything seemed quiet, too quiet. The street I was on was totally silent. I couldn't even hear any traffic noises from the interstate just a few hundred yards away. I clicked on the radio, fiddled with the station selector, but I only got static. There was only one other car in sight, and that was an old one, a really old one, like an antique, parked in front of a diner named 'Henry's.'

"When I hit the intersection, I had a funny feeling, like moving through cool water. But from that point on, I saw all right. I knew where I was, and that was just where I should have been all along.

"Now I have driven that route a couple of thousand times, and I had never seen a diner named 'Henry's.' I asked around at the mill, but no one had ever heard of a diner with that name in the whole city.

"My question is, did I somehow drive into another dimension that night, some kind of alternate universe? Or did I drive down that street the way it might have been thirty or forty years ago?"

If the man was actually driving down a street that had existed in that same city several years before, where did the present-day street go? If the past returns, what happens to the present? Can both exist at once?

And what would have happened if he had run over and killed someone from the earlier time period? Can someone from the present interact with someone from the past?

It seems that in the most carefully documented accounts of trips into the past, the inhabitants of the earlier time period take no notice of those from the present. Perhaps the observer does not actually step "into" the past. Instead, it seems that a scene from the past is recreated in precise, photographic detail, as if some ethereal movie were being shown for an audience of one.

8
Spooklights
and Fire Devils

In the little town of Silver Cliff in the Wet Mountain
Valley of Colorado, ghostlights have plagued the
local cemetery since 1880. According to local folklore, the lights were first seen by a group of miners
passing the cemetery after a festive evening at one
of the local taverns. When they saw the flickering
blue lights over the gravestones, they swallowed
their laughter in sober gulps, tossed away their bottles, and left the area in a hurry.

Since that night in 1880, the lights have been
watched by generations of tourists and residents of
Custer County, and reported in the *Wet Mountain
Tribune* in the spring of 1956, and in the August
20, 1967, issue of *The New York Times*.

Skeptics have suggested that the curious blue
lights are only a reflection of houselights in the valley. But County Judge August Menzel said that he
remembered well the night when everyone in Silver
Cliff and nearby Westcliff shut off their lights. Even

the streetlights were turned off, Judge Menzel recalled, "but the graveyard lights still danced."

If the ghostly cemetery lights aren't the reflection of ordinary house and municipal lights, just what might they be? Old-timers and younger speculators have come up with many theories over the past one hundred years:

1. The ghostlights are reflections from the stars and the moon. *But the lights are just as clear on starless, moonless, cloudy nights. In fact, the darker the night, the brighter the lights.*

2. The ghostlights are created by hoaxsters with luminous paint or some other glow-in-the-dark materials. *But no evidence has ever been found to support such a charge.*

3. The ghostlights are caused by radioactive ores. *But Geiger counters testing the entire area have discovered no trace of radioactivity.*

To add to the confusion, the strange blue lights can never be approached for a closer examination. As soon as anyone comes too near, the lights seem to disappear — only to pop up again in another section of the cemetery. Photographers have been hired to capture the lights on film, but none of them has been very successful.

Many of the old-timers in the area are amused by efforts to explain away the lights as due to unknown, but *natural*, causes. According to these elderly folks and the legend that they repeat, the old graveyard became the final resting place for many miners who died while scraping precious ore out of the mountain valley. The old-timers say the flickering globes of the ghostlights resemble the lights worn on the miners' caps. Legend has it the eerie lights are the restless souls of the miners who still search for the treasures they never found in their lifetimes.

Spooksville's Steady and Dependable Ghostlight

A notorious ghostlight is located in the tri-state area of Spooksville, where the corners of Missouri, Arkansas, and Oklahoma come together. Spooksville's ghostlight is so dependable that it is advertised as a tourist attraction, and it annually brings in hordes of curiosity-seekers.

In appearance, the Spooksville ghostlight resembles a bright lantern. On many occasions the light dims before spectators, then bounces back in a brilliant blaze of light. Hundreds of firsthand encounters with the mysterious ghostlight are on record.

During World War II, the U.S. Corps of Engineers scoured the entire area, using the latest scientific equipment available. For weeks they explored caves, tested mineral deposits, and staked out highway routes. They seem to have exhausted every possible explanation for the origin of the mystery lights. The engineers finally left, confounded.

In *Spooksville's Ghostlights*, a small pamphlet written and published by Bob Loftin, such accounts as the following two reports are included.

Louise Graham said that a spooklight perched on

the rear window of a school bus as it returned from a school carnival in Quapaw, Oklahoma. Every child in the bus was convinced that the spooklight was attempting to enter the vehicle, and they were all terrified.

"The light was so bright," Ms. Graham said, "that it temporarily blinded the bus driver, and he had to stop the bus. Just as we stopped, the light went away."

Chester McMinn, of Quapaw, told of the night when he was plowing after dark beause it was so intolerably hot during the day. "Seems the old spooklight felt real neighborly that night and decided to help me with my plowing. I couldn't see too well, and I guess the old spooklight sensed it, because he started hovering all over the field where I was plowing."

McMinn said that he appreciated the spooklight's neighborly concern until it suddenly darted in his direction. The farmer says that he "absolutely froze stiff" on his tractor until the light drifted out of sight.

As with the graveyard lights in Silver Cliff, Colorado, many people have tried to solve the mystery of the Spooksville ghostlight. There are the expected folk legends of ghosts, goblins, and the restless spirits of long-dead Indians, as well as the standard scientific explanations of reflected moonlight, hoaxes, and misinterpretations of natural phenomena.

The present spooklight area seems to focus on a dirt road some eleven miles southwest of Joplin, near the Missouri-Oklahoma line. The light, according to the thousands who have witnessed it, is seen almost every night from a half hour after sunset to a half hour before sunrise. It varies in intensity and time of appearance, and sometimes breaks up into distinct pairs of lights.

One serious investigator found that the spooklight appeared most often to float just above the hills down the roadway to the west. At rare times it seemed to come toward the observer. Through a telescope, the investigator claimed to have perceived as many as four distinct pairs of lights, with pairs of red lights appearing slightly to the right of pairs of bright white lights. The red lights grew dimmer as the white lights became brighter.

Many researchers have believed that they have discovered the answer to the spooklight enigma when they have taken note that U.S. Route 66, running east and west from Commerce to Quapaw, Oklahoma, is in direct line with the spooklight road. They suggest that lights from cars and trucks could be bent, or refracted, out of their normal paths and could appear to be bouncing balls of fire on the dirt road twelve miles away. The bright white lights appearing slightly to the left of the dimmer red lights would correspond with the natural movement of traffic on a highway.

Area residents admit that this explanation seems to fit perfectly. The problem is, the spooklight has been seen in the area since 1903 — and that was long before cars streamed along Route 66.

In his position as curator of the Spooksville Museum, L.W. Robertson was quoted as stating that he had no idea what the spooklight could be. "I've looked at it about as much as any living man," he said. "It is here for people to see for themselves. I accompanied the U.S. Army Engineers on the experiments to explain away the light in 1946. Maybe the old Indian and Civil War legends are just as plausible as the scientific theories."

Meeting the "Luz Peculiar"

Writer-fisherman Bill Mack described his investigation of the mystery light of Bahie Kino, a Mexican Gulf of California resort, for the June, 1970, issue of *Fate* magazine. He stated that his first introduction to the *luz peculiar* occurred when a strange bluish light came through the windows of his camper-trailer and awakened him one night at about 10:00 P.M.

The light appeared to be about fifty yards long, and Mack estimated that its brightness extended about twenty-five feet in the air. "There it sat," he commented. "Just a blob of blue light!"

While he was exploring the area thoroughly, trying to find a clue to the light's source, he learned that the mysterious light had been seen so often and for so long a time period that it had been greatly feared by the Seri Indians who had inhabited the area long ago. Mack also discovered that a research team from the University of Arizona had spent three days in the area, probing, digging, and testing with an assortment of instruments. Their unofficial conclusion was that the *luz peculiar* resulted from the ionization of the air that occurs only under specific conditions. They could not explain, however, why the ghostlight appeared only in the one spot.

About a month later, on his third research trip to the area, Mack watched the light begin to glow at about 11:00 P.M. on a quiet, sultry night. The ghostlight remained visible for nearly two hours that night, and Mack observed it carefully. He had reasoned that if the ionization theory was correct, then perhaps something large and metallic might be the cause. He believed there could even be a meteor just beneath the ground surface.

"Like everyone else's, my efforts were doomed to failure," Mack conceded. "Neither my compass nor my metal detector were affected in any way by the ghostly glow. . . . Maybe the Seri Indians are right, and the light is a spirit. From what I've been able to figure out, they have just as much evidence as any of us other investigators."

Ball Lightning Tries to Hijack a Soviet Airliner

In January of 1984, a Soviet Ilyushin-18 airliner left the city of Sochi on the Black Sea. At first the weather was excellent for flying, but not long after takeoff, the crew sighted thunderclouds about sixty miles from the craft's flight path. Then, according to *Tass*, the Soviet press agency:

"Suddenly, at the height of 1200 yards, a fireball about four inches in diameter appeared on the fuselage in front of the crew's cockpit.

It disappeared with a deafening noise, but re-emerged several seconds later in the passengers' lounge — after piercing in an uncanny way the airtight metal wall.

"The fireball slowly flew about the heads of stunned passengers. In the tail section of the airliner, it divided into two glowing crescents, which then joined together again and left the plane almost noiselessly."

Tass stated that although no damage was done to the interior of the plane, there were two holes in the fuselage. The pilots were able to turn the plane around and land it safely without further incident. Passengers and crew had survived an encounter with "ball lightning," one of nature's rarest and eeriest phenomena.

Dr. Leonard Reiffel, a syndicated science writer, once made an appeal to his readers for their personal experiences with ball lightning. From their responses, Reiffel found descriptions of the size of ball lightning ranging from as small as a golf ball to as large as three or four feet across, "the most common being described as the size of a basketball or grapefruit."

Many people informed Reiffel that they had seen a ball of lightning come through a closed window, then, within seconds, materialize on the other side of the glass. The science writer suggested that, if the ball passes through a screen, this ability may be electrical phenomenon, "metal being a good electrical conductor."

Can Fire Exhibit a "Devilish" Intelligence?

On the night of January 4, 1967, the J.W. Curlee family of Indio, California, barely managed to escape with their lives when their house caught fire and burned to the ground. When the ashes had cooled, there were three mysteries connected with the blaze that none of the Curlees could explain.

First, when they opened the family safe, they discovered blackened, melted, and fused coins, but the birth certificates of daughters Cheryl and Sharon, eighteen-year-old twins, had escaped the melting heat caused by the flames.

Second, the day after the fire, a picture of the baby, David, was returned to the Curlees by fire investigators. Although the frame and the glass were gone, the photograph was not even scorched.

And third, most inexplicable of all, was when Mr. Curlee returned to work, he found the shoes that he had set at his bedside on the night of the fire neatly awaiting him alongside his desk. The leather showed no sign of flames, and Curlee was completely unable to explain how the shoes got to his office.

The Curlees' story demonstrates the strange twists that fires may take in their flaming paths of destruction. There are recorded instances of fires that mysteriously avoid certain articles while all else is reduced to ashes. Fires have broken out in one corner of a room and then seem to have chosen to burn only certain items.

Unexpected flames have been caused by mysterious fireballs and, on other occasions, fireballs have bounced about rooms without causing any damage at all.

A Fire Devil in the Dresden Library

In December, 1968, flames suddenly erupted in the Dresden, East Germany, public library. The fire was restricted to fourteen shelves, which were totally demolished. Inches away, volumes under a different classification remained untouched. The only books consumed were the library's complete collection of volumes on witchcraft and evil sorcery.

The Night the Santa Catalina Mountains Did Not Burn

On the night of February 8, 1955, a huge conflagration in the Santa Catalina Mountains was observed from the streets of downtown Tucson, Arizona. As people gathered to watch, individuals in the crowd estimated that the flames were climbing skyward to a height of fifty feet. The blaze continued unabated for nearly eight hours.

The next day, a search party composed of deputies, air rescue teams, and journalists moved into the mountains in search of the site of the fire. After a long period of time, the searchers finally located an area some 3,700 feet up that they knew had to be the correct spot. The enigma was that there was almost no evidence that a fire of any significant size had occurred, certainly not one as large as the one witnessed the night before. There were some large rocks scorched black that jutted out of the landscape, but there were no patches of ashes anywhere, and there were no charred remains to corroborate the account of a great fire in the Santa Catalinas.

Something very weird had occurred in the mountains, though, for several cacti in the vicinity were found to have crystallized, and certain areas of soil were found to be scorched three to four inches deep. Although no one knows precisely what occurred that night in the Santa Catalinas, some peculiar kind of burning did take place.

A Mysteriously Inflammable Dress

Another inexplicable fire occurred inside the Charles H. Williamson home in Bladenboro, North Carolina, on a January morning in 1932 when Mrs. Williamson's dress suddenly burst into flames. Her husband and teenaged daughter tore the burning dress from her body, and when all had recovered from their shock, they were astounded to see that Mrs. Williamson's body was unharmed. Stupefied, father and daughter examined their own hands. Neither of them had suffered a single burn, blister, or even the slightest singe.

9
The Terror of Spontaneous Human Combustion

On March 26, 1965, a friend who had come to visit seventy-year-old Herbert Shinn, of Camp Chaffee Road, Foster Park, California, found him in his kitchen with severe burns on his chest, back, and spine. He died thirty minutes later in a hospital.

Shinn had been alone when the friend had discovered him, and investigators found absolutely no evidence of fire anywhere in his house or in his yard. Nothing in his house had burned. But deadly flames had ended Herbert Shinn's life.

In December, 1956, Mrs. Virginia Caget, of Honolulu, Hawaii, walked into the room of seventy-eight-year-old Young Sik Kim to find him enveloped in blue flames. By the time the firemen arrived on the scene, Kim and his easy chair were ashes. Strangely enough, nearby curtains and clothing were untouched by fire, in spite of the fierce heat that would have been necessary to consume a human being.

On August 19, 1966, Doris Lee Jacobs, of Oceano, California, burned to death in her trailer home. Although Ms. Jacobs suffered burns on over ninety-five percent of her body, the inside of the trailer was only partially scorched. Officials could offer no explanation for the fire because it was the woman, not the trailer, that had burst into flames.

On January 8, 1974, Andrew Jackson Huckabee was walking along a road outside of Ramer, Tennessee, when he was seen to erupt into flames. Although he was rushed to Jackson-Madison County General Hospital, the dying man was never able to give medical personnel the slightest clue as to how he had been so suddenly transformed into a human torch.

In December, 1965, Mrs. Katherine Elizabeth Chaires was discovered on fire in the living room of her apartment on Liberty Street in Oneida, New York. Edward Wilcoxon, who lived in the same building, burned his hand trying to remove Mrs. Chaires from the flames.

On December 9, 1956, the Boston *Sunday Globe* reported that Mrs. Catherine Cahill, seventy-eight years old, an invalid Roxbury widow, died in a mysterious blaze that was confined to her rocking chair.

On September 20, 1938, at Chelmsford, England, a woman burst into flames in the midst of a crowded dance floor. No one was able to extinguish the blaze that seemed to be fed by her own flesh. In minutes, she was but a heap of ashes.

"In all my experience," Coroner Leslie Beccles

said after he had conducted a thorough investigation, "I have never come across any case as mysterious as this one."

What terrible unseen forces bring about the deadly blue tongues of fire that consume human beings?

Spontaneous Human Combustion Most Often Claims Female Victims

It appears that spontaneous human combustion is sexist, for there is little question that women are most often its victims.

On July 30, 1937, a woman who had been paddling about in a small boat with her husband and children in England's Norfolk Broads was engulfed by terrible blue flames and, in a matter of a few horrifying moments, was nothing but a mound of ashes. Neither the boat nor any member of her family was harmed.

Journalist Charles Fort, collector of "damned" happenings that remain puzzles to science, considered that "spontaneous human combustion" might actually be caused by "things or beings, that with a flaming process, consume men and women, but like werewolves, or alleged werewolves, mostly pick out women."

The following incidents were reported in 1931 in Fort's book, *Lo!*:

• Barbara Bell, seventy-seven, was found on a sofa with her body burned as if it had been a long time in the midst of intense flames.

- Mrs. Thomas Cochrane, of Rosehall, Falkirk, England, was discovered burned almost beyond recognition, but her charred body was surrounded by pillows and cushions that showed not the slightest sign of fire.
- Elizabeth Clark was found covered with burns in an unscorched bed.
- Dr. B.H. Hartwell, of Ayer, Massachusetts, was called to observe the crouched form of a woman being consumed by flames coming from her own flesh.

Dr. Thurston's Conclusions Regarding Spontaneous Human Combustion

In a 1961 study, Dr. Gavin Thurston studied the literature of spontaneous human combustion and came to such conclusions as the following:

1. Under certain conditions a body will burn in its own fat with little or no damage to surrounding objects.
2. The combustion is not spontaneous, but started by an external source of heat.
3. Such combustion has occurred where the body has been in the path of a draft up a chimney from a lighted fire. Oxygenation is good, and the pull of the flue prevents outward spread of the fire.

In order to test Dr. Thurston's theories, Dr. Gee, a lecturer in forensic medicine at the University of Leeds, England, conducted a number of experiments. He learned that human body fat, when melted in a crucible, will only burn at temperatures somewhere near 250 degrees centigrade. However, a cloth wick prepared in liquid fat will burn even when the temperature of the fat has dropped as low as 24 degrees centigrade.

Dr. Gee also enveloped a layer of human fat in several folds of thin cloth in order to produce a roll about eight inches long. Combustion of the roll proceeded slowly along its length, burning with a smoky yellow flame and producing a great deal of soot. In both of these experiements, a fan was arranged so that combustion would proceed in a direction opposite to the flow of air.

Dr. Gee admits that these experiments are by no means conclusive, but he argues that they support the theory put forward by Dr. Thurston, "which seems the most reasonable explanation for the occurrence of these curious phenomena."

But reasonable explanations do not always fit the actual circumstances and the facts of a situation.

More Victims of the
Terrible Burning Death

Some years ago, Joan Hart found her invalid sister Mary sitting in a parlor rocking chair literally swathed in flames. Joan snatched up a throw rug and wrapped it around Mary in order to smother the flames.

Somehow Joan managed to carry her sister upstairs where she laid the badly burned woman on a bed with clean sheets. But while Joan went to get help, Mary "caught" fire again. When Joan returned with a doctor, Mary had been reduced to ashes — with the exception of her head and some fingers.

Amazingly, the bedclothes were not damaged in any way. There was only that strange coating of greasy soot that is reported in so many of these cases.

On April 7, 1969, sixty-year-old Mrs. Grace Walker, of Cedar Avenue, Long Beach, California, was found on the floor of her living room with burns covering ninety percent of her body. Although she was still alive when discovered, she was pronounced dead on arrival at the hospital.

Investigating police officers said that the only signs of fire in the house were the ashes left from Mrs. Walker's clothes, which had been burned from her body by the flames from her flesh. There were no burners ignited on the stove, and not a single match was to be found in the house. Friends and relatives emphasized the fact that Mrs. Walker did not smoke, and that she never carried matches.

Dr. J. Irving Bently, a retired physician living in Potter County, Pennsylvania, had received guests on the evening of December 4, 1966; but on the next evening, a visitor ran from Dr. Bently's apartment "white as a ghost" and shouting to the neighbors, "Dr. Bently is burning up!"

Investigators found what was left of the elderly doctor in the earthen basement beneath his bathroom. All that remained of the man was a heap of ashes, the lower half of one leg, and his nearly unrecognizable head. Nothing else in the bathroom had burned, and the physician's aluminum walker with its rubber-tipped legs were unaffected by the mysterious fire. The paint on the bathtub — just inches from where the flames had burned a hole in the floor — was not even blistered.

Is Ball Lightning Responsible for the Mysterious Cremations?

In 1960, Mrs. Louise Matthews, of South Philadelphia, survived an eerie experience that might offer an explanation for at least some of the mysterious spontaneous combustions.

Mrs. Matthews claims that she was lying on her living room sofa when she glanced up to see a large red ball of fire come through both the closed window and the venetian blinds without harming either. At first Mrs. Matthews thought that a nuclear bomb had fallen, and she buried her face in the sofa.

But the ball of fire passed through the living room, into the dining room, and drifted out through a closed dining room window. Mrs. Matthews said that it made a sizzling sound as it floated through her house. She telephoned her husband at work, told him the strange tale, and asked him to come home at once.

Matthews may have suspected that his wife was overwrought about something and had had some vivid dream or imagined the whole episode, but when he walked through the front door, he began to weep. His wife had proof of her experience. When he had left for work that day, she had a full head of hair — now she was half bald!

Louise Matthews stated that she had felt a tingling sensation in the back of her head as the ball of fire passed over her. She felt the spot with her hand, and discovered her hair had fallen out, leaving her scalp as smooth and clean as her face.

Rose Howe, of New Braintree Road, Barre, Massachusetts, was not so lucky. On July 16, 1960, alerted by her screams, Mr. and Mrs. Arthur Drake, who lived upstairs in her home, ran down to find Mrs. Howe's clothing aflame from her waist up. Later, the investigating authorities could not find any reason why the woman had suddenly become a living torch.

Spontaneous Human Combustion in a BBC Television Studio

On October 14, 1974, British television actor Derek Boote was all dressed up in a space monster costume and waiting to go on camera for the filming of a Welsh-language children's space comedy at the BBC's studios in Cardiff, Wales. When screams were heard from his dressing room, rescuers rushed in to find the actor in flames.

Although the crew members eventually were able to beat out the fire, Boote was terribly burned and taken to the hospital in critical condition. Neither he nor anyone else on the set could offer any explanation for the sudden explosion of flames.

Unseen Flames Consume a Man and His Pets

On March 23, 1975, William Cashmore, age eighty-two, died in a fire in his home in Walsall, England, along with his dog and his parakeet. Investigating officials inspected the gas and electrical appliances and found everything in order. The only signs of the fire were in Cashmore's clothing and in the chair in which he had sat. The victim, a nonsmoker, had been sitting near his pet bird with his dog at his side when he apparently erupted into flames.

Strange Accounts of Human "Flamethrowers"

A letter from surgeon Stephen Power of the Royal Homeopathic Hospital, London, to the British Medical Association's *Journal* told of a real-life "flamethrower." According to Dr. Power, every time a certain British clergyman bent to blow out the altar candles, his breath caught fire. Although it might be temporarily effective to breathe a bit of fire and brimstone into one's sermons on certain occasions, it certainly would be an awkward condition on an extended basis.

Dr. Power informed his colleagues that the cause was found to be a buildup of an inflammable gas in the patient's stomach caused by a duodenal ulcer. After an operation, the surgeon stated that "the person was able to carry out his duties in a more decorous fashion."

On May 20, 1878, the *Glasgow News*, Glasgow,

Scotland, reported a series of bizarre fires in farmers' haystacks that always seemed to occur when twelve-year-old Ann Kidner passed by. She was never seen to go near the haystacks, but she may not have needed to touch them. Strange as it may seem, the human mind may be capable of focusing enough raw energy to cause objects to burst into flames.

It was reported in Toronto, Canada, in December, 1891, that a fourteen-year-old girl named Jennie Bramwell was seen to go into a trance and, by pointing at ceilings or walls, cause them to crackle and blaze with fire.

In 1929, there was a teenaged girl in the West Indies who simply could not be kept in clothing. Whenever she put on a new dress, it began to smolder and burn. She always received the oldest bedsheets because her parents never knew when her covers might catch fire upon contact with her flesh. The girl herself never had any burns on any part of her body.

Just How Much Heat Does It Take to Convert a Human Body to Ashes?

Just what kind of heat must be generated to reduce a human body to ashes in a matter of minutes? Some years ago, Dr. Wilton Krogman, professor of physical anthropology at the University of Pennsylvania, intrigued by the bizarre reports of spontaneous human combustion, conducted several experiments regarding the effects of fire on flesh and bone.

Dr. Krogman tested bones still covered in human flesh, bones without flesh but not yet allowed to dry out, and bones that had dried. He burned cadavers in a wide variety of fires fed by such combustibles as hickory and oak, gasoline, coal, and acetylene.

First and foremost, Dr. Krogman learned, it takes a terrific heat to completely consume a human body, both flesh and skeleton. Once he watched a body in a crematorium burn at 2000 degrees Fahrenheit for over eight hours, burning under the best possible conditions of both heat and combustion, with everything controlled. Yet at the end of that time there was scarcely a bone that was not still present and completely recognizable as human.

Dr. Krogman commented, "Only at over 3000 degrees F. have I seen a bone fuse so that it ran and became volatile. These . . . are very great heats that would affect anything flammable within a considerable radius of the blaze."

How, then, in the cases of spontaneous human combustion, could human beings burn beyond recognition — sometimes in a matter of minutes — yet not cause the fire to spread beyond the chairs in which they were sitting, or beyond the small area of the floors on which they sprawled? According to Dr. Krogman, the temperatures required to bring about such combustion should ignite and consume anything capable of burning "within a considerable radius of the blaze."

The Extraordinary Case of Mrs. Mary H. Reeser

In what has become a classic case of spontaneous human combustion, Mrs. Mary H. Reeser, of St. Petersburg, Florida, was last seen relaxing comfortably in an armchair in her apartment at 9:00 P.M. on Sunday evening, July 2, 1951. When a telegram was delivered to her eleven hours later, nothing remained of the 170-pound woman but a shrunken skull, one vertebra, and a left foot wearing the charred remains of a black slipper.

The windows of Mrs. Reeser's apartment were open all night, yet no one smelled anything burning or saw any smoke.

The apartment itself, though terribly warm, was almost completely unharmed. The rooms were coated with oily soot above a four-foot line only. The armchair, lamp, chairside table, and a small portion of the carpet directly beneath the armchair were destroyed. Nothing else was damaged.

Mrs. Reeser's skull had shrunk to the size of a baseball. In tragedies in which humans are consumed by intense heat, the skull normally expands, sometimes even explodes.

Fire Chief Nesbit said that he had never seen anything like the case in all his years of investigating fires. Edward S. Davies, arson agent for the National Board of Underwriters of Tampa, Florida, stated that they "just don't know what could have caused it."

A spokesperson for a St. Petersburg mattress

company pointed out that there was not enough material in any overstuffed chair to cremate a human body. The basic stuffing is cotton, often combined with felt and hair or foam-rubber cushions. None of these materials is capable of bursting suddenly into violent flames, although they are able to smolder for long periods of time.

Dr. Krogman remarked that he could not conceive of such a complete cremation without more objects having caught fire and burned in the apartment. "Unless the woman was burned elsewhere and the remains placed back in the apartment, I am baffled and amazed," he admitted.

At first Dr. Krogman believed that a "superlightning bolt" might have struck Mrs. Reeser, her body serving as a conductor to ground the current through a wall-type heater behind the chair. But he discarded this theory as soon as he learned that local weather bureau records showed no lightning in St. Petersburg on the night Mrs. Reeser met her horrible and bizarre death.

"Never have I seen a skull so shrunken or a body so completely consumed by heat," Dr. Krogman remarked. "This is contrary to normal experience, and I regard it as the most amazing thing that I have ever seen. As I review it, the short hairs on my neck bristle with vague fear. Were I living in the Middle Ages, I'd mutter something like 'black magic.' "

Police Chief J.R. Reichart received an FBI report that stated, "There is no evidence that any kind of inflammable fluids, volatile liquids, chemicals, or other accelerants had been used to set the widow's body ablaze."

Spontaneous human combustion remains a mystery, striking without warning and without leaving a clue.

10
Animals That Talk, Spell, and Find Their Way Home

Because she has used her college degree in psychology to work with disturbed cats, rather than maladjusted humans, Manhattan psychologist Carole Wilburn has become known as "the Kitty Freud." In more than twenty years as a cat counselor, Ms. Wilburn estimates that she has helped more than 10,000 frustrated or frightened felines.

"Actually people and cats are not all that different," she explained to journalist Susan Fenton. "Cats feel happy, sad, anxious, and frustrated, just like humans."

Indeed, there is growing evidence that animals feel and *know* more than most of us have previously believed.

Feats of the Remarkable "Lady"

A little over sixty years ago the extraordinary feats of what was an apparently ordinary horse became a major topic of conversation for millions of

Americans. Lady, a three-year-old mare, owned by Mrs. C.D. Fonda, of Richmond, Virginia, seemed to be able to read, work complicated problems in mathematics, and communicate with human beings. Lady was thoroughly studied in 1928 by Dr. J.B. Rhine, the famous parapsychologist from Duke University, and Dr. William McDougall, a leading psychologist. For over a month the two scientists carefully conducted a most amazing series of tests with the seemingly gifted black and white horse. The scientists were attempting to determine if Lady really could accomplish all of these unhorselike stunts. And she proved to be quite a success.

Even with Mrs. Fonda removed from the scene and with a screen placed between the horse and the experimenters, Lady was able to pick out numbers in answer to arithmetic problems and to select alphabet blocks to spell out words in response to conversational questions.

By nudging forward the correct blocks, Lady was able to carry on a simulated dialogue with anyone who desired to question her. Her rapid, consistently correct answers led Dr. Rhine to conclude that some animals were able to read the thoughts of humans through some extrasensory capacity.

In a *New York Times* article of May 28, 1928, the writer noted that it seemed a bit unkind to declare Lady a telepathic horse. "This makes it seem," he pointed out, "that Lady performs her miracles merely by mind reading, whereas the investigations might well prove that she understands English and arithmetic on her own account."

The Accomplishments of "Clever Hans" and His Arabian Friends

English is not the only language of horses. Karl Krall, of Elberfeld, Germany, had three horses that animal psychologist Dr. Edward Claparede of the University of Geneva, Switzerland, pronounced "able to perform many of the tasks which are required of an intelligent schoolboy of fourteen."

Krall's horses were able to count, add, subtract, multiply, use decimals, read, spell, and respond to questions in a simplified language that he had developed for them to use to communicate. During one test, when the horses were asked to give the cube root of 5,832, one of the horses stamped out the correct answer — 18 — while university scholars were still figuring out the solution on paper.

In 1909, Krall had inherited a horse named Clever Hans from Wilhelm Von Osten, a man who firmly believed in the high intelligence of animals and who had taught Hans a wide variety of skills. Krall had come to accept Von Osten's theories, and he immediately bought two Arabian stallions to train. One of the horses seemed naturally skilled in mathematics, while the other showed a definite preference for language and spelling.

Such a controversy developed in France, Germany, and England over the true abilities of the trained horses that a commission was appointed to investigate the intellectual capacities of the Elberfeld stallions. Dr. Edward Claparede, one of the leading European authorities on animal psychology, concluded that the horses were not fakes and that they did read and spell and extract cube roots by "rational processes rather than by means of trick signs from their trainer."

Dr. Claparede emphasized that he could find "nothing whatever to the idea that [Krall] signals the horses either consciously or unconsciously."

A Dr. Hamel once gave Muhamed, one of the Arabian horses, the number 7,890,481 and challenged the animal to produce its fourth root. Within 6 seconds, Muhamed had tapped out his answer, 53. Dr. Hamel checked with a table and was astonished to find that the horse was correct. It requires 18 multiplications, 10 subtractions, and 3 divisions to extract the fourth root of a 7-figure number. Muhamed had managed those 31 calculations in 6 seconds.

In July, 1955, Dr. William MacKenzie, of Genoa University, president of the Italian Society of Parapsychology, was asked if he remembered the Elberfeld horses. "Could I forget!" he answered immediately. The only explanation that Dr. MacKenzie could offer was that the horses were "mediums," possessed by a reasoning mind greater than their own.

Geoffrey Cowley, in the May 23, 1988, issue of *Newsweek*, points out that there was more to the story of Clever Hans and Wilhelm Von Osten. A young psychologist named Oskar Pfungst made the discovery that although Hans succeeded on nine out of ten problems if the interrogator knew the answers, his score plummeted to just one out of ten if the questioner was ignorant of the correct sum:

"Further studies showed that [Hans] had learned to read minds, by monitoring subtle changes in their posture, breathing and facial expressions. So keen was his sense of these cues that informed questioners couldn't conceal them if they tried. Hans could always tell when it was time to stop tapping or moving his head."

In his article "The Wisdom of Animals," Cowley concludes that "even scientists who don't like to speculate about consciousness are parting with the old notion that animal behavior consists entirely of reflexes. There is too much evidence that animals live by their wits."

And what of Muhamed and Clever Hans? "[Scientists] are acknowledging that while Clever Hans might not have learned math, the knowledge he displayed was awesome just the same."

Tantalizing Tales of Talking Animals

And what about animals that *talk*?

Syndicated columnist Ann Landers once published a letter from a woman who insisted that she heard a neighbor's poodle asking to be let outside. Ms. Landers was at once flooded by mail from readers who said that they, too, had talking pets.

Here are excerpts from some of the letters:

"We have a thirteen-year-old rat terrier who says, 'I want out.' "

"Our dog says, 'Howdy, partner,' 'Vas you dere, Cholly?' and 'Good-night all.' It all started when our dog, Heinz, sneezed, and my husband said, *'Gesund-*

heit!' We almost fell over when Heinz repeated after him, '*Gesundheit!*' "

"Our schnauzer speaks Italian. He says, 'Mamma Signora.' "

Pepe the Chihuahua Sends His Love

Some years ago on a spring day, Rudy Gallucci was called to fix the furnace at the Genova residence in Torrance, California. "Will your dog nip me?" he asked Mrs. Genova, warily eying the small Chihuahua sitting on the porch. Gallucci had been bitten before by dogs that appeared friendly.

Mrs. Genova assured him that Pepe had a gentle disposition. The repairman took his customer at her word, and walked down to the basement with the Chihuahua at his heels.

"Well, how are you, Pepe?" he asked, wanting to test the dog's true spirit before he turned his back on him and got to work.

"Hello, how are you?" came the reply in a high-pitched voice.

Gallucci's mouth dropped open, his eyes blinking in astonishment.

"I love you," Pepe added.

"I could feel my hair rise," Gallucci said later to a reporter for a local trade newspaper. "I was actually looking the dog square in the eyes. I saw his mouth open and heard the voice coming out of it."

The repairman picked up the dog and laughed. "I love you," Pepe said again.

Gallucci thought that perhaps an operation of some kind had been performed on the dog, "sometimes like people do to crows to get them to talk like parrots."

But Mrs. Genova laughingly assured him that Pepe could talk. She even allowed Gallucci to take the dog back to his office to entertain his coworkers.

It wasn't long before Pepe and Mrs. Genova were local celebrities. She told others who came to investigate that she had first heard Pepe say, "I love you-oo" one day as she was hanging some things out to dry on the clothesline. She called for her husband to come outside, and the dog mouthed, "How are you? How are you?"

Pepe had been examined by veterinarians who theorized that the extra length of his palate and the peculiar formation of his larynx, combined with his flexible throat muscles, might enable him to produce the sounds of human speech. Some observers also noted that Mrs. Genova spoke to Pepe with exaggerated mouth and tongue movements.

When one investigator bent down close to watch the dog's throat muscles move, she saw Pepe's tongue curve toward the roof of his mouth, as if he were making a conscious effort to form syllables. Such a tongue movement is most unusual. Dogs generally keep their tongues down on their lower jaws when making sounds.

Dogs That Play the Piano and Type Messages

Mrs. C.K. Wilderson, of north Denver, claims to have a dog that plays the piano. The Denver *Post* described Tramp as an eleven-year-old ham performer that took to the keyboard at the slightest encouragement. Many observers have seen Tramp stride to the piano, sit down, and begin to bang away with both paws. The dog appears to keep time with its tail and yowls lustily in "song."

Alan McElwaine, of the London *Sunday Times*, wrote of a dog named Arli that seemed to have mastered the keyboard of a typewriter, becoming a literary, rather than a musical, pooch. Arli was a six-year-old English setter owned by Mrs. Elizabeth Mann Borgese, daughter of the late Nobel Prize-winning author Thomas Mann.

According to the article, the setter used its nose to punch out words of up to four letters. Arli didn't just spontaneously display a talent for writing. Mrs. Borgese admitted that she had laboriously taught her pet to hunt-and-peck at the keyboard. Arli had begun with "dog" and "cat," and worked up to "bone," "go bed," "bad dog," and so forth.

Barking His Way Through Arithmetic

A fifteen-month-old cocker spaniel with the awesome name of Ginjo Roughneck Sweettooth Chester (Dog-Dog for short) was able to bark out the answers to arithmetic problems, according to his owner, Earl W. Chester, of Sacramento, California. Chester put Dog-Dog through his paces for David Deas of the Sacramento *Bee*, and the journalist gave the dog's arithmetic an "A."

Chester told the reporter that Dog-Dog's ability was not an act. "It's a psychic phenomenon," he said. "How does Dog-Dog understand what I'm saying to him? We haven't been able to figure it out. He knows these things already, and it is just a matter of studying it and bringing it out."

April to the Rescue

April, a three-year-old terrier-Chihuahua, appeared to be completely illiterate, but she more than earned her keep by saving the lives of the humans around her.

Mrs. Eddie Baker, of Gallup, New Mexico, April's owner (or perhaps April sees it the other way around), stated that she was awakened one night by the dog and was led into a son's bedroom to find the boy hemorrhaging and choking on blood. Thanks to April's summoning her to the scene, Mrs. Baker was able to save her son's life.

A few months later, Mrs. Baker was led outside by the barking dog and directed to an old refrigerator. When the puzzled woman pried open the door to investigate, she found her seven-year-old son unconscious and near death from asphyxiation.

Incredible Accounts of Pets
That Found Their Way Home

Then there are the remarkable stories of animals, such as Lassie in the classic tale, that always manage to find their way home.

Blackie, a fifteen-pound black Persian cat that had been accidentally left in Florida by Mr. and Mrs. Richard Bower during Thanksgiving of the year before, found its way back to their home in Forked River, New Jersey.

A dog named Smokey found its owners, Mr. and Mrs. Phillip R. Bean, of Seattle, after having been separated from them for three and a half years — and after the Beans had moved *twice*.

The Saga of Baby, the Dognapped Spaniel-Poodle

Baby, a cocker spaniel-poodle mix that suffered from epileptic seizures, managed to find its way back to the John Donegan family of Addison, Illinois, after having been "dognapped" somewhere for eight months. To complicate matters for Baby, the Donegans had moved to Addison from Melrose Park, so the dog first had to find the trailer house of Mrs. Donegan's mother to appeal for help.

In recounting the story for the Chicago *Tribune*, Donegan said that the dognappers were probably puzzled when Baby had one of her epileptic fits. "They didn't understand what it was, and they threw her out."

Mrs. Donegan's mother lived over fifteen miles from the Donegans' new home, but Baby had visited "Grandma's" house with the family before she had been dognapped.

Mrs. Donegan said that Baby looked terrible when she arrived at her mother's trailer. "Her nose was sunburned and swollen, her feet were raw, and two back teeth were broken. But it was our Baby! She still had her dog tags on. Now our family is back together."

Hector, the Dog That Stowed Away
to Yokohama to Find Its Master

What about the fantastic story of Hector, one of the greatest of all the pets-that-came-home tales?

Second Officer Harold Kildall of the S.S. *Hanley* was busy seeing to the loading of cargo on the morning of April 20, 1922, when he saw the black and white terrier walking up the gangplank. The dog paced about on deck, sniffed at various objects, then returned to shore on the Government Dock in Vancouver, Washington.

From time to time that day, Kildall noticed the large terrier inspecting the four other ships at dock. He was intrigued by the dog's air of having a genuine purpose. But he was too busy to pay the animal more than casual attention, for the *Hanley* was getting ready to ship out.

The next day when the ship was on its way to Yokohama, Second Officer Kildall was surprised to discover that the big black and white terrier had somehow managed to stow away aboard ship.

Fortunately for Hector, Captain Warner liked dogs and didn't sentence the terrier to be thrown overboard as food for the sharks. Both he and his crew made the terrier welcome.

Although Hector was willing to work for his fare — he stood watch with Second Officer Kildall each night — he remained aloof, refusing to express any true affection toward the crew members.

Three weeks later, the S.S. *Hanley* was unloading timber in Yokohama Bay. Kildall could not help noticing the terrier's behavior as their vessel pulled up next to the S.S. *Simaloer*, a Dutch ship that was also unloading timber. Two officers and some crewmen from the Dutch ship boarded a small boat and began to move toward the customs landing. As they passed close to the *Hanley*, Hector began to leap about and bark excitedly. At the same time, one of the passengers in the small boat spotted the big terrier and began to wave his arms and shout.

Within moments, Hector was reunited with his master, W.H. Mante, second officer of the *Simaloer*. The man and his devoted dog had been separated at the Government Dock in Vancouver, and the Dutch ship had sailed away before Mante could find Hector.

How was the big black and white terrier able to select the one ship among all those at the dock in Vancouver that would take him across the ocean to the precise spot where his master would be waiting?

A Real-Life "Dr. Doolittle"

And now we turn our attention to a former wrestler, Marine jujitsu instructor, sharpshooter, champion swimmer, and merchant seaman who became a real-life "Dr. Doolittle." Fred Kimball was able to "talk" to the animals, and they "talked" back.

"I don't really *talk* to animals," Kimball once explained, referring to his frequently demonstrated ability to calm and apparently communicate with troubled domestic and wild animals. "I focus on their minds with mental telepathy."

Kimball would admit that it was a bit strange to

be able to read the mind of a sea gull, for example. "Of course, most of the time they don't think too much," he said.

Once a group of observers were amazed when Kimball "talked" a gopher out of its hole by offering it a yellow flower. First he tried to bargain with it to emerge by offering it some grass — but the gopher held out for the yellow flower that was just too far away from its hole to fetch in perfect safety.

The rodent ate the flower from Kimball's hand and retreated only when a four-year-old boy got a bit too close. "He [the gopher] said he didn't trust the boy," Kimball explained. "He said the boy was too young to be responsible for his actions."

Once a friend of Kimball's in Florida needed some money in order to get married. Kimball talked to the horses at Hialeah racetrack and picked fourteen winners out of the seventeen races.

"You can't always win them all," he said, shrugging off the three losses. "The horse may be on the level, but he may not have a good rider."

Several years ago, Kimball was with the Army Engineers in Panama, chopping roads through the heavy jungle. "I seemed to have a 'jungle instinct,' as they called it," Kimball recalled. "I could sense when poisonous snakes were too close, so they made me point man. That meant I was out in front with the snakes.

"We had snakes that hung in foliage at about the level of a man's head. One strike from them, and a fellow didn't have long to live. Some men were so unnerved that they'd start to cry. Because I could sense the snakes before we could see them, the men felt safer with me up front."

Kimball maintained that pets are able to store up vast memory banks, and it is this information that he tapped. It wasn't difficult to speak with a dog, he said, because they use basic terms. When he communicated with them, he used symbols in order to learn their problems and complaints.

"Dogs often complain because their masters do not demand enough of them," Kimball once remarked. "Dogs like to be trained and active. Some even become a bit bored with their human family."

He cautioned dog owners that when a dog appears merely to be sleeping in front of a warm fireplace or the television set, they really have both ears tuned into family relations. And what is more, dogs can remember things that happened to their human family in the past.

"The animal has in its memory certain things that the owner may have forgotten." Kimball explained. "The animal gives me a mental picture of what it wants to say, and then I 'translate' it for people. The language of animals is very much like the language of children."

The Teenaged Boy Who Lived on the Back of a Giant Stingray for Sixteen Days

Kimball always insisted it is within each person's own heart that he or she will find the ability to "talk" to animals.

Shipwreck victim Lotty Stevens must have had

his heart tuned into the giant stingray that carried him on its back for sixteen days and even drove off killer sharks that tried to attack him.

Eighteen-year-old Stevens's incredible adventure began on January 15, 1990, when he left Port Vila, Vanuatu, in the South Pacific, to go fishing. A raging storm set in, which capsized his boat and drowned his companion. For three days, he clung to the overturned boat; then, with only a lifejacket for support, he tried for two days to swim to land.

The teenager continued to pray for a miracle, fighting to keep away fear and despair. Then he got his miracle.

With his eyes still closed, he felt something big lift him from the water. There beneath him was a giant stingray, at least eleven feet long (including the six-foot poisonous tail), taking him on a "marvelous magic-carpet ride."

At first Lotty was frightened, he admitted to journalist Chris Pritchard. "But I soon began to think of the stingray as my friend. I patted it like a dog. Its skin was slimy, but its body felt hard and strong."

After several days aboard the stingray, the creature suddenly dove and disappeared. Lotty then saw an enormous shark coming straight for him. Then he saw a second shark — and a third.

Suddenly his "angel" reappeared, swimming in a fast circle around him. The sharks turned and swam away. Once again, Lotty Stevens had been saved by the stingray, and he climbed back on board its strong body.

The teenager survived by catching fish from atop his friend until the wonderful morning when he sighted land. The stingray headed for the shallow water, and tipped Stevens off near the beach.

Lotty remembers staggering like a drunken man, then collapsing on the sandy beach. The next morning he was awakened by a fisherman, and he realized that he didn't get a proper chance to thank his friend from the ocean.

A hospital on the main island pronounced Lotty in good shape except for some dehydration and a few sores from salt water and chafing against the life jacket. When he telephoned his family, their grief turned to joy, for they had already held a funeral service for him. Over and over, Lotty Stevens said, he gives thanks to God for the wonderful stingray that saved his life.

11
Fairies, Elves, and Little Men from UFOs

"I was born and reared in Norway," wrote my correspondent, "and until about nine years ago, I lived there. All of my life I have loved to take long walks in the fresh air, either in the daytime or in the early evening." The letter went on to recount a strange tale.

"One evening I was out walking in a remote region in the north of Norway, feeling very much at peace with the world. A full moon had just risen, and the beautiful night had just turned a dark lavender. I had been walking for perhaps a mile when I came upon a makeshift bridge across a brook. As I was crossing the bridge, I suddenly saw in the distance something that looked like a little boy running toward me.

"As he came closer, I saw that it was not a boy at all, but what appeared to be a midget dressed in a brown leather coat and leather trousers. He also wore black buckled shoes.

"He ran up to me, and for no reason that I could fathom, jumped upon me. Needless to say, I was totally unprepared for this attack. He pinned me down, and small as he was, he had the strength of an ox.

"After a long and desperate struggle, I finally freed myself.

"When I had regained my feet, he suddenly turned tail and ran toward the brook. It was then that I saw the strangest sight that I had ever beheld. The little man vanished as if the earth had swallowed him up. I searched for hours around that spot, but I could find no trace of the weird, combative little man. Since that night, I have believed in Trolls, Gnomes, and Elves."

Never Plant a Pole in a Fairy Mound

A group of Irish workmen found that one should *not* cross the Wee People, not even in the twentieth century. The trouble began when the workmen began digging a hole for an electric-power pole in a small mound outside of Wexford, Ireland. The villagers warned the workmen that the mound was a "rath," or dwelling place, for the Little People.

When the townspeople told the workmen that the pole would never stay in place, the electricians were quick to scoff at such childish superstitions — the very idea, suggesting that "fairies" could dislodge a pole they had so expertly sunk into the mound of earth! They would have a hard time of it, indeed, if they tried to pry loose a pole that hearty workmen from the state electricity board had set in place.

The next morning, however, the large pole tilted awkwardly in loose earth.

"Those flaming idiots," the foreman scowled toward the village. "So they think they can have a bit of fun with us with their flaming fairies, eh? Look here, lads, some of the fun-loving clods crept out here during the night and wiggled the pole loose."

The foreman ordered the pole reset with an extra bit of tamping.

The next morning, the pole again rested loosely in churned-up earth. Other poles in the line stood straight and firm, but the pole that invaded the fairy rath tilted to the side.

The foreman decided that he had had enough of the game the practical jokers in the village were trying to play with him. He ordered the hole to be dug six feet wide. Once this had been accomplished, he placed the pole precisely in the middle and packed the earth so firmly around its base that he thought nothing short of a nuclear blast could hope to loosen it.

When dawn came, the workmen knew they were defeated: The pole had been thrown completely free of the Wee Folks' rath.

Ignoring the knowing grins of the villagers, the workmen dug a second hole four feet outside the perimeter of the fairy mound. The pole still stands there today, solid as a rock.

Negotiating with the Hidden Folk of Iceland

In 1962, some enterprising gentlemen in a small village in Iceland decided to enlarge a herring processing plant. According to Icelandic tradition, every landowner must reserve a small plot of his property for the mysterious "Hidden Folk." A few of the local people pointed out to the plant owners that any extension of the processing works would encroach on the plot of ground that had been set aside for the Little People.

The businessmen laughed. They possessed modern, unbreakable drills, plenty of dynamite, and a highly qualified crew to operate the equipment. Progress would not be held up by such a ridiculous superstition.

But as soon as the work had begun, the "unbreakable" drill bits shattered one after the other. An old farmer came forward to repeat the warning that the drillers were trespassing on land that belonged to the Hidden Folk.

The workmen merely laughed at the man. But the drill bits kept right on breaking.

Finally, the manager of the plant, although he refused to believe in such nonsense as "Hidden Folk," agreed to the old farmer's suggestion that he consult a local seer to establish contact with the Hidden Folk of the area and attempt to make peace with them. The seer went into a trance state and told the manager that there was one particularly powerful Hidden One who had selected this particular plot as his special dwelling place.

The Hidden One was not unreasonable, however. After the seer had carefully explained that the businessmen truly needed the extra area for the expansion of their plant, the entity agreed to find another place to live. The Hidden One asked only for some time to make his arrangements. If the manager would cease drilling for five days, the entity would have enough time to find another plot of ground.

The manager felt more than a little strange negotiating with something that he could not even see, but he glanced at the pile of broken drill bits and told the seer that the Hidden One had a deal.

After five days had passed, the workmen resumed drilling. From then on, the work went efficiently, without incident. Not another "unbreakable" drill bit was broken.

Clap Your Hands if You Believe in Fairies!

Such tales sound as if they come from a time long ago. But whatever strange powers the Little People had over their human neighbors in centuries past seem to be just as strong today. What were, or are, the Wee People?

They may have been the surviving remnants of a past civilization and a species of small humans. Such Wee Folk may have been quite advanced and may have possessed technology that seemed magical to the migrating barbarians who later moved into the area. The Wee Ones may have died out, been assimilated into the encroaching culture, or they may have gone underground.

In most traditions, especially in the British Isles and Scandinavia, the fairy folk inhabited magical kingdoms beneath the surface of the earth. Fairies have always been considered to be very much akin to humans, but they have also been regarded as something more than mortals. As many of the ancient texts declare, the fairy folk are "of a middle nature betwixt Man and Angel." One factor has been consistent in fairy lore: The fairies, or "middle folk," continually meddle in the affairs of mortal men and women, sometimes for good, sometimes for evil.

Sir Arthur Conan Doyle and the Controversial Cottingley Fairy Photographs

In the December, 1920, issue of *Strand* magazine in London, several allegedly genuine photographs of fairies were published, and the controversy over their authenticity continues to this day. The pictures were said to have been taken with a simple, inexpensive camera by two young girls, Elsie Wright and her cousin Frances Griffiths, near the village of Cottingley.

The famous author of the Sherlock Holmes mysteries, Sir Arthur Conan Doyle, managed to obtain the negatives and brought them to one of England's most eminent photographic analysts. At first the man laughed at the whole idea of fairy photographs. However, amazingly, he ended up making a public statement saying that he was quite willing to risk his professional reputation, but he could find not even the slightest evidence of fakery in the pictures.

Striving to be as thorough an investigator as his fictional detective hero, Sir Arthur brought the strange negatives to the Kodak Company's offices in Kingsway. The experts there declined to go on record that the girls had actually photographed fairies, but they did issue a statement that they could find no evidence of trick photography, or of anyone having tampered in any way with the film. They also emphasized that they could find no flaws of any kind on the negatives.

A third photographic analyst observed that while such effects might have been created by some very clever studio artist, the most significant factor in the Cottingley photographs was that the fairy figures had actually been caught in motion.

The controversial photographs had been taken in a little valley with a narrow stream running through it. Elsie Wright met the fairies first, and she introduced them to her cousin at once. One snapshot taken by Elsie in the summer of 1917, when she was sixteen, captures her ten-year-old cousin seated on the grass surrounded by a group of four dancing fairies. Another, taken a few months later, shows Elsie with a tiny gnome.

As the press spread the story of the Cottingley photographs around the world, many reputable individuals came forward to testify that they, too, had played with the Little People as children. More elaborate and more expensive cameras were sent to the girls in the hope that they might snap some additional photographs. And according to Elsie, Frances, and others, images of fairies did show up on the plates of the more sophisticated cameras.

Sir Arthur Conan Doyle enlisted the services of one of England's most gifted clairvoyants to see if he might be able to psychically verify the two girls' accounts of fairies in the little valley. The clairvoyant sat down with the girls in the lovely natural setting and found that he was able to see even more than they because of his paranormal abilities. He found that the entire glen was alive with many different forms of life — wood elves, gnomes, fairies, goblins, and even undines, or water nymphs, floating over the stream.

But the clairvoyant said that he wasn't able to "feed" the fairies enough psychic energy for them to materialize. It appeared, however, that both Elsie and Frances had this amazingly rare ability.

Sir Arthur issued a summary of his investigation in which he stated: "For the present, while more evidence will be welcome, there is enough already convincing evidence available."

The Continuing Folklore of the Wee People

Call them fairies, brownies, leprechauns, or elves, an enormous library of folklore has been built around stories of the Wee Folk.

According to Scottich and Celtic legend, fairies are the counterparts of humankind in "person, occupations, and pleasures, but unsubstantial and unreal, ordinarily invisible." The Wee Folk possess magical powers, but they are mortal, though leading much longer lives than humans. Nevertheless, tradition has it, the fairies are strongly dependent upon humans and seek to strengthen their own race by kidnapping human beings. They are of a nature between spirits and men, but they can intermarry with humans and bear children.

The Native Americans were also familiar with the Wee People who inhabited field and forest, and the northeastern tribes called them the *Puckwudjinies*. This is an Algonquin name that signifies "little vanishing people." What is especially thought-provoking is that *Puck*, of the Algonquin dialect, is exactly the same as Puck of British fairy traditions, the woodland elf who appears in Shakespeare's *A Midsummer Night's Dream*.

Puck is also related to the German *Spuk*, a goblin, and the Dutch *Spook*, a ghost. Then there is the Irish *pooka*, and the Cornish "pixie." *Puck* is no doubt derived from the old Gothic *Puke*, a name for minor spirits in all the Teutonic and Scandinavian dialects. To break down the Algonquin *Puckwudjini* even further, we find *jini*, the Arabs' *jinni*, or genie, the magical entity of the wish-granting lamp.

Wee People from Other Worlds, Other Universes

The fairies are said to enchant humans in order to take advantage of them. They seem to delight in kidnapping children and adults and whisking them off to the underground fairy kingdom.

On the other side of the coin, stories are told of the fairies helping a farmer harvest his crop or a housemaid clean up a kitchen or a shoemaker finish mending shoes. They have on occasion guided humans by divining the future, and have stood by to assist at the birth of favored children and remained to tutor and protect them for the rest of their lives.

It is interesting to consider how many of the previous references to fairies are quite similar to modern accounts of humans allegedly interacting with UFO occupants. The UFOnauts have been reported to hypnotize or "enchant" men and women. In such books as Whitley Steiber's *Communion* and Budd Hopkins's *Missing Time*, there are accounts of Earthlings being taken on board a UFO in order to try to create a hybrid species. There are many well-documented cases in which men, women, and children claim to have been kidnapped and taken aboard UFOs, just as people of an earlier time were taken to the fairies' magic kingdom. And extraterrestrials have been reported working closely with certain humans throughout the years, aiding and advising them.

Perhaps the most widely known bit of fairylore is that in which a farmer comes upon Wee Folk digging in the earth. The farmer naturally assumes that the little ones are burying their gold, so he grabs one by the leg and forces him to tell of his hidden treasure. This done, the farmer frees the elf and marks the spot so that he will be able to find it again. By the time he returns with his tools, the spot has been altered in some manner to make digging up of the gold an impossible task.

But perhaps the "fairies" are not digging for or

burying their gold at all. Perhaps the Little People are UFOnauts taking soil or mineral samples, and do not wish their true activities known.

Notice how the following account of an alleged kidnapping by UFOnauts might have been told as an encounter with the Wee Folk if it had occurred in an earlier time period.

The Miner Who Had the Misfortune to Interrupt Wee Folk at Their Digging

On August 17, 1962, Rivalino da Silva, a miner from Diamantina, Brazil, came upon two strange little people, each approximately three feet tall, digging a hole in the earth. Startled, the tiny men ran into the bushes at da Silva's sudden approach. While the amazed man stood rooted to the spot, a hat-shaped fiery object ascended into the sky.

Da Silva went home that night and probably tried to put the whole weird business out of his mind. The next day when he told his friends at the mine what had happened and what he had seen, they laughed at him.

Shortly after dawn on August 20, Rivalino's twelve-year-old son Raimunda was awakened by strange voices. He swore later that he heard the voices say, "Rivalino is in here. He must be taken."

Raimunda saw a shadow of something — not quite like a human being, and only half as large — float, rather than walk, through his bedroom.

Then his father began to move as if entranced. He opened the front door and walked toward two large globes that hovered about six feet off the ground. The strange objects made a humming sound and blinked with an eerie kind of light.

Raimunda screamed at his father to come back into the house, but Rivalino continued to walk toward the mysterious floating globes. Before the boy could make a move to clutch his father by the hand and shake him out of his peculiar trance, the objects had emitted a heavy, yellowish smoke that completely enveloped his father.

When the smoke cleared, the floating balls had disappeared — and so had Rivalino da Silva.

Raimunda and his young brothers, Fatimo and Dirceu, ran sobbing to the police station, crying out the unbelievable tale of their father's disappearance. Aware only that something very bizarre had occurred at the da Silva home, the police began an immediate investigation.

The investigating officers found a strange, cleanly swept area in the dust about sixteen feet in diameter. They could find no sign of any footprints or tracks in the area. The officers did find a few drops of blood about 160 feet from the house, but even though laboratory analysis established the fact that it had come from a human, they were unable to prove conclusively that the blood was da Silva's.

Police tried to crack Raimunda's story, on the premise that the boy had murdered his father and somehow found an ingenious method of disposing of the corpse. At last they became convinced that the terrified twelve-year-old sincerely mourned his lost father and was psychologically incapable of murder.

At about the same time, a fisherman came in with

a story that he had seen peculiar globes circling the da Silva home on the evening of August 19. Da Silva's miner friends reported that he had told them about his encounter with the two weird little men. The case was officially closed, labeled as "unsolved."

Place this story in an earlier place and time and a different cultural context, and you have the classic fairy tale of a workman who comes upon two Wee Folk burying their gold. After he fails to trick them into giving up their treasure, the man is whisked off to the fairy kingdom, never to be seen again.

Even the descriptions given by men and women who claim modern UFO encounters match those given of the fairy folk, who stand between three and five feet tall, have large eyes, a pointed chin, and very small features.

Could the romantic tales of dancing fairies and woodland elves be ancient accounts of UFOnauts as interpreted by storytellers of long ago in the language and technology of earlier times?

A solid kernel of very strange reality may lie at the core of hundreds of years of *supposed* myth and legend, like a great, confused, cosmic ball of string. And if that great ball is ever unraveled, it just might take humans from Earth to the stars!

About the Author

BRAD STEIGER has been called one of the most popular writers on the subject of unexplained phenomena. He is the author of over one hundred books for adults, including *Hollywood and the Supernatural*, *Monsters Among Us*, and *Ghosts Among Us*. His work has also appeared in a number of magazines, such as *Parade* and *Alfred Hitchcock's Mystery Magazine*. A former teacher and editor, Mr. Steiger lives in Scottsdale, Arizona.